# Interwoven Love

## The Beautiful Fabric of Love in Marriage

### Gabriel Tew

RIVER BIRCH PRESS

Mesa, Arizona

ISBN 978-1-956365-86-3 (print)
ISBN 978-1-956365-87-0 (e-book)

For Worldwide Distribution
Printed in the U.S.A.

River Birch Press
P.O. Box 7341, Mesa, AZ 85216

# Table of Contents

# 1

## A Love Story

Ben, the fabric designer, had tried every possible ratio of the four yarns to get the combined color exactly to Mrs. D'amore's satisfaction. Or so he thought.

"I have one more idea." Mrs. D'amore suggested. "Is it possible to intertwine the red thread with each of the other threads, essentially making the color ratio three parts red, one part blue, one part yellow, and one part white, with each of the other colors wrapped in red?"

"That would actually be a ratio of four reds to one of each of the other color threads. Yes, we could do that, although I've never seen it done exactly that way."

"Wonderful! We're trying to create a unique fabric, so it stands to reason it would require the first ever thread ratios, doesn't it?"

"Yes, ma'am, I suppose it does."

"When can we see the test run?"

"I'll have the crew do the interweave tonight, and we'll run it through the loom first thing in the morning."

"Great! I'll be here at ten to see the results."

## [10:00 The Next Morning]

"Now that's what we've been looking for!" Mrs. D'amore finally now held in her hand the fabric she'd seen in her mind's eye months before.

———◆———

David had proposed to Angelina twice, and twice Angelina said no. She wasn't convinced that David understood marriage or love well enough to enter into a committed lifelong marriage relationship. Heeding Angelina's charge that he needed to understand what love is, David recently read a book titled *Interwoven Love*. He now believed he was prepared for marriage and planned to propose a third time, this time hopefully successfully.

We drop in on David and Angelina as they're taking a romantic walk on a mountain trail. They stop at a park bench, and David turns to Angelina.

"I love you so much." David peered into Angelina's eyes with such piercing passion that he could almost see her soul.

"Can you be more specific?" Angelina still doubted her boyfriend meant love in the correct sense.

"More specific?" David was caught completely off guard, hoping things would go better this time; he'd hoped for the response, *I love you too, David.*

"Yes, more specific. What do you mean by love?"

"Well, I hope you can see that I've made a lot of changes, completely rearranging my whole life—my character, my priorities—all for you."

"I can see that, and I'm so touched by it. Still, I wonder if, by *love*, you really mean *want*."

"Yes, *want* is the right word," David said, "I do want you but not in a selfish way. I want you so I can show you how precious you are to me…and to God.

"I want to show you patience, that I'll never give up on you. I want to show you the gentle kindness I feel toward you in

2

my heart. I want to serve you before my own needs and reject any unfavorable ideas toward you.

"I want to show you that I'll protect you, trust you, believe in you, always be there for you. I want to never let you down.

"So, yes, I guess loving you is wanting you but in these ways, not just so I can have my selfish desires satisfied by you. And yet I know that if you'll accept my love, my desires will be met; loving and serving you in these ways is what I want. It is my desire.

"I want to be best friends with you, to lead a household with you, to be intimately connected with you spiritually, emotionally, and sexually in a way that brings both of us great joy and satisfaction. I want to be intimately connected with you—only you.

"That's specifically what I mean by loving you. I do want you very much. I love you very much, Angelina." David gently lowered Angelina's hand, helping her join him on the park bench as he sat down.

"I have to say that was definitely the right answer." Angelina smiled at David as they sat together.

"In that case," David lowered himself onto his left knee and held up a small black box, opening its lid and revealing a brilliant diamond ring, "Will you marry me, Angelina, and be my forever love?"

Angelina was elated. The joy of having David grow in his knowledge of love, doing it all for her, and say it to her so poetically; yes, this was the man for her.

"Yes! Yes! I will spend my life as your wife, and I will love you in the same ways you have vowed to love me. I love you too, David!"

*There's the response I was looking for!* David thought.

Angelina was blissful and impressed by David but still

curious as to how he'd become so well versed in love. "When did you get so wise about love?" she asked.

"Well, to be honest, I read a good book on the subject recently." David smiled. But his inner smile was so much bigger than the one he showed to Angelina.

## [One Week Later]

Mrs. D'amore walked in the front door of her home, excited to present her son, David, with her gift. She found him in the kitchen getting dinner started. Dad was almost home, and Angelina would be there in a half hour, so David worked quickly to have it ready on time.

"I have an engagement present for you and Angelina." Smiling her biggest smile ever, David's mom set the gift bag on the counter in front of David.

"Shouldn't I wait for Angelina? You know, she's joining us for dinner tonight."

"Yes, of course. Of course. Maybe I can wait that long. I'm just so excited!"

"I'll just put it over here near the table." David placed the bag behind the chair where he would be sitting.

"That was delicious!" Angelina declared as she finished the last of the wine in her glass and looked at David, so impressed with his skills in the kitchen. "How often can I look forward to meals like that one?"

"Good question, Angelina," said Mrs. D'amore. "I believe that's the first meal of David's I've ever had, and it only took twenty-six years to get it."

She laughed, and David's dad poked him on the side of the shoulder.

"I don't want to over-promise," David said as he reached

back and picked up the gift bag and set it on the table. "But now, the moment Mom's been waiting for—she's given us an engagement present."

David reached in and lifted a beautiful red blanket out of the bag. As he stood and spread it out, everyone could see the writing on the blanket: *Interwoven Love*.

"It's beautiful!" Angelina was overcome with gratitude at being so warmly welcomed into David's family. "I don't think I've ever seen that exact color before."

David's mother was impressed that Angelina noticed. "It may be the very first ever fabric of that color. I created the thread ratio just for you two; of course, it took me months of experimenting."

"But, Mom, we just got engaged last week."

"I just had a strong feeling it was coming. And I didn't settle on the message on the blanket until after you read that book, and Angelina said yes."

Angelina held her tears back and finally spoke with a shaking voice, "It all came together so perfectly."

"Yes, it did," David agreed as he leaned over, lifted Angelina's chin, and gave her a soft kiss.

# 2

## Love = x

Communication about love has often been confusing to me. As a young man in my teens and into my twenties, my understanding of love was the one purveyed by pop culture. I believed it was a feeling, something that happened to you if you were lucky. It was passion, desire, attraction, something you wanted someone you felt that way about to have for you. I never gave it much thought and never was exposed to anything different.

When I was growing up, my mom would say I love you to me and each person in our family, but I was always uncomfortable by her saying it, so I never said it back. I had close friendships, but I would never have thought of those relationships as love; friendship wasn't love.

I did find myself drawn to the love ballads of music artists of the seventies and love affairs involving an attractive girl on TV or at the theater. And, like most boys my age, I was keenly interested in beautiful girls and women, like Melissa Sue Anderson from *Little House on the Prairie* and the *Charlie's Angels'* actresses. Pretty girls at school and elsewhere captured most of my adolescent attention, and I carried that same interest through my high school years and into college. To me, the greatest possible love situation was to have mutual, strong romantic feelings of attraction with a beautiful girl who also had other deeper qualities of character and personality.

During my junior year in college, I surrendered my life to Jesus. However, nothing really changed in my understanding of what love was, except the ideal girl for me, now, would possess the additional quality of being a serious follower of Christ.

One Friday night during my senior year, the campus ministry showed a video on the subject of love. I went, mainly because the video was being played in the lobby of one of the girls' dorms. The video was a teaching by Josh McDowell, whom I had never heard of, but whose teaching opened my eyes to a very different idea of love. Josh said love isn't just a feeling; it can be accompanied by feelings, he said, but it's more than that. He taught that love is a choice and an action.

**Love can be accompanied by feelings, but it's more than that.**

While Josh helped me greatly in my journey to understand love, there was still so much I didn't know about it because I didn't understand that there was more to it. I now knew that love is a choice and an action and that it may come with feelings but isn't, itself, a feeling. That was all I knew, and I felt satisfaction that I was now knowledgeable about love. But my satisfaction was ill founded.

As a seminary student and serious student of the Bible, I learned that the Greek language, in which Scripture was written in the time soon before and after the earthly life of Jesus, has four words, all of which are translated into the one English word *love*. I soon realized a major reason for my confusion was that *love* in the English language is a variable. So, when someone used the word "love," they likely meant one of the four Greek loves or some other type of love, but due to the single word limitation, their meaning was unclear and unde-

# The English word love is a variable.

fined—a variable. I understood the Greek words, but could there be even more loves than the four? Could it be there are even more types of love than the Greeks identified? Could there be an undefined number of loves? At least the Greeks came up with four types, a far cry from the grossly inadequate single word we English speakers have.

As I say, I realized that the English word *love* is a variable (love = x). When we use it, what does it really mean? In my frustration, I set out to discover or create a theorem to help solve for x. The goal is that, in conversations about love, both the sender and receiver of the idea of love understand clearly and are on the same page. The book, *The 5 Love Languages* by Gary Smalley, has been a big help to me and millions of others. While Smalley's book established a system to understand how love is communicated, a void still existed in my understanding as to what *type* of love we may be communicating in a given scenario.

I decided that there must be a way to define the variable, to solve for x. That's one way of stating what this book is all about. Ideally, upon completion of this relatively short read, your conversations about, and understanding of love will be much clearer, particularly as love pertains to marriage. My hope is that you'll be able to solve for x, to know specifically what love means in a particular situation.

As we define x in our ideas of love—whether communicated or thought—I hope we can also use that understanding, as we apply it to marriage, to maximize the quality of our marriage relationships. It has helped me greatly to recognize the different loves my wife and I have for each other, and to be aware of which type of love we should recognize as appropriate at various times.

If we're to have a clear understanding of life's mathematical mysteries, variables must be solved. We learn algebra in school to learn to solve certain mysteries. Of all of life's mysteries, marriage has been one of the most difficult ones to solve. With the understanding this book offers, we can solve the mystery and walk in the fullness of marital love. Pardon the pun, but that's the value (get it? Because we want the value of x?) of *Interwoven Love*. As we solve the mystery, we will know the value of love—or the loves—in marriage.

# It's Greek to Me

"It's Greek to me"—the cliché phrase for when we don't understand something at all. Many of us would say that about marital love. It's Greek to us; we don't understand it at all. Ironically, the best way to understand love in marriage is to learn the Greek language's influence on the meaning—or meanings—of love.

> **A marriage relationship, as God intends it, will include all four types of love.**

There are four Greek words that represent four different types of love. Only two of them were used in Scripture; the other two are found only in other Greek writings. A marriage relationship, as God intends it, will include all four types of love. As unique as marital love is, so also is the arrangement of these four love-types.

The first step in understanding how the four Greek loves relate to marriage, however, is learning the meaning of each of the loves.

## Agape Love

God used the quills of Paul and John to define the kind of love He has and *is* for people—*agape*. In preparation for understanding agape love, my advice is to memorize the following two passages of Scripture; they contain the most essential points of agape's meaning.

10

*Love is patient,*
  *Love is kind.*
*It does not envy,*
    *it does not boast,*
      *it is not proud.*
*It does not dishonor others,*
    *it is not self-seeking,*
      *it is not easily angered,*
        *it keeps no record of wrongs.*
*Love does not delight in evil but rejoices with the truth.*
*It always protects,*
  *always trusts,*
    *always hopes,*
      *always perseveres.*
*Love never fails.*
1 Corinthians 13:4-8

*Dear friends, let us love one another, for love comes from God.*
*Everyone who loves has been born of God and knows God.*
*Whoever does not love does not know God, because God is love.*
*This is how God showed his love among us: He sent his one and*
*only Son into the world that we might live through him. This*
*is love: not that we loved God, but that he loved us and sent*
*his Son as an atoning sacrifice for our sins. Dear friends, since*
*God so loved us, we also ought to love one another. No one has*
*ever seen God; but if we love one another, God lives in us and*
*his love is made complete in us* (1 John 4:7-12).

We memorized the 1 Corinthians 13 passage as a family when all our kids were ages four to thirteen, more than twenty years ago, a fun and memorable time, and I've been thankful many times since then that those verses are hidden in my heart. It provides an exhaustive list of agape's characteristics.

Embedded in the 1 John 4 passage, on the other hand, are three major truths about agape:

1. Agape love comes from God. It cannot originate with us; it came from Him and still comes from Him.

2. Agape love is expressed to us through Jesus, God's Son, sent to earth. The best way to really understand agape is to know and study Jesus.

3. We are extenders of agape love. We aren't mere recipients or have reservoirs that store up God's love for us; we are to relay on to others what we have received from God. If agape is WIFI, God is the provider (ISP), Jesus is the router, and each of us is the extender.

As you read this book's contents about agape, you'll process them very quickly, naturally, and thoroughly if these two sections of Scripture are stored in your heart through memorization. Moreover, if these truths are readily accessible to your perspective and are a permanent part of your mentality, your decision-making about and treatment of your spouse will be more naturally godly and loving.

I'll save further unpacking of these Scriptures for later chapters; for now, please let it suffice to memorize these words of the Apostles Paul and John.

## Phileo Love

There is a special love that friends have for one another— the Greek phileo love. By comparison, agape is in Scripture hundreds of times, phileo, dozens, and the other two none. We could speculate as to the reason, but the most obvious inference is that God wants us to love everyone as friends and with the type of love He has for us, agape, remembering that He calls each of us His friend.

Many people, myself included, can tend to make things comparable and competitive when they shouldn't be. I have six kids, and I wanted to teach them that I could love each of them to the max without loving any of them less; so, as they were growing up, I would say to each of them, "You're my favorite." The first few times, they looked at me like this was our little secret and they had a bigger place in my heart than their siblings did.

But eventually, after some comparing of notes with their brothers and sisters, they realized I was saying the same words to all my them. But what I wanted to teach them, and what they soon realized, was that *favorite* didn't have to be exclusive. I think they finally got it, if not before then, when I wrote and sang them a song called *My Favorite*. (Search *Gabriel Tew My Favorite* on YouTube.)

That said, there is one person that should be our very best friend, closer than any other person in the world.

More will unfold in the chapter on Phileo, but please understand the most basic principle of friendship for a complete marriage—our spouse comes before all other friends. If this isn't true for you, troubles await you.

## Storge Love

Family members share a special love for one another. For the ancient Greeks, this love was called *storge*. Husband and wife are not only best friends but also family members. They form the nucleus of the nuclear family. The way they love each other is critical for the family's wellbeing and success.

## Eros Love

Of the four loves, *eros* least fits into the marriage fabric God has designed. The English word "erotic" comes from the Greek eros. To get an idea of eros, consider our culture's use of the word. The dictionary definitions all pertain explicitly to sex; while sex was created by God for good reasons, one dictionary's list of synonyms of erotic includes vulgar, smutty, racy, foul and perversive. These words indicate what our culture—and the world at large in all its history—have done with God's wonderful gift. So, to reclaim sex and romance for godly use, it must be made godly, which will be covered in the *Eros* chapter.

# 4

# The Love in Marriage Theorem

$$x = a + ab + ac + ad$$

*x represents marital love*
*a represents agape*
*b represents phileo*
*c represents storge*
*d represents eros*

Although this chapter and the previous one come relatively early in the book, I'm writing them last. My wife reviewed the first draft manuscript that didn't include these chapters. Despite some others being far more experienced and skilled at editing than she, Sharlene is my most valued voice at some stages of my writing process. It was the same when I had weekly preaching responsibilities. I could always rely on her to help me see what adjustments I needed most in communicating God's Word effectively.

After reading the first draft, Sharlene thought I needed more clarity near the beginning about what the four loves are and how they work in a basic, practical sense. So here's my stab at it. Hopefully, it'll be pleasing to Sharlene and helpful to you, the reader, although I feel safe in saying the mathematical analogy would not be her choice method for making the interwoven idea clear. But different minds work in different ways.

The equation approach fits my thinking and, hopefully, won't mess it up for our readers.

As the equation above indicates, marital love is not simple but complex. Simpler would be one variable. Every married person knows marriage is neither simple nor easy.

In reality, married love includes a total of eight love variables—x, a, b, c, d, ab, ac, and ad. The good news is that all eight are definable, as stated above in what each single variable represents, so marriage can be simplified by solving its love variables. Once the love variables are solved, the x factor (marital love) is defined. And we understand marital love more thoroughly as we understand the other parts of the equation—all the Greek loves and their stated combinations. In the ensuing pages, we'll come to understand what the equation means in real-life terminology that we can apply to marriage.

### a represents agape

Notice that *a* is the most abundant of all the characters in the equation. Agape is the most important of all factors in having a complete marriage. This love must exist in marriage if the other factors are going to be effective, each spouse embracing agape and proactively applying it to their spouse.

Being proactive with agape love is important. It means:

1. memorizing its primary Scripture passages,

2. having it anchored in our hearts so as to be part of our mentality concerning our marriage, and

3. carrying it out with our actions.

We should also use agape reactively. Reactive is often used as a bad word, implying we, instead, are proactive, getting ahead of potential problems rather than simply reacting once they've occurred. But with agape love, we must be both proactive and reactive, as such traits as...*is patient...not easily angered...keeps no record of wrongs*...exist for responding to something from someone, namely in marriage, our spouse.

Obvious in the equation is the need for agape as a multiplier of the other love types, so understanding agape is as vital to completing the marital love equation as mastering the number two is to grasping the square root concept. For non-math-lovers, it is as vital as recognizing the color red so you can choose it and add it to blue to create purple. In case both of my analogies are failing, the point is that we need to understand agape love very well so we can intertwine it with the other loves in marriage. One last analogy—before we can start baking a cake, we need batter ingredients; agape would be the flour.

### b represents phileo

I see phileo as the second most important type of love for spouses after agape. In other words, spouses should have a very, very strong friendship. (I'm resisting the temptation to delve into friendship with greater detail, since the *Phileo* chapter will do just that.)

### c represents storge

Spouses of a complete marriage will love each other as the family members they are with one another. Again, there's much more to it, but we'll patiently wait until the *Storge* chapter for its deeper meaning.

### d represents eros

Of the four loves, eros, the sex and romance love type, is least able to contribute to a good marriage independently, without agape's being intertwined with it. More on that in its respective chapter, too.

**ab means that agape is being applied in the friendship of the spouses**
Having agape as an integral part of our attitude catapults our friendship to epic satisfaction levels.

**ac is agape being given and received in the family relationship spouses have with each other**
It shows up in real life as all the agape traits being expressed to each other as the husband wife lead the family together.

**ad is the married couple enjoying sex and romance love (eros) with all the agape traits guiding its expression**
To have d without a, or eros without agape, will lead to catastrophic hurt and regret for married couples.

In summary, I offer three pieces of advice to help make the theorem work in real married life.

1. Make agape your life's philosophy. Agape is the same thing as grace, God's way of fixing our relationship with Him and the best way to manage the marital relationship.

2. Love your spouse with all the loves, with the priority being in the order, agape (favor without requirement), phileo (friendship), storge (family), then, eros (sex and romance).

3. Remember that all the loves work best in tandem with agape and that eros works not at all without its partnership with agape.

Finally, it may help to memorize the theorem, especially if you tend to think logically or mathematically.

$$x = a + ab + ac + ad$$

# ~5~

# Love's Fabric in the Life of Jesus

God could have orchestrated the timing of the coming of the Messiah to coincide with any culture in history. Yet, in His limitless ability to control the timing of things, He chose ancient Greek culture into which to send His Son. First century Palestine was a multilingual culture of Jews, Romans, and other Gentiles, most of whom spoke Greek in addition to the languages of their respective subcultures. Jesus probably spoke Greek plus His Galilean dialect of Aramaic, in addition to Hebrew. The timing of the Messiah being in Israel and His church being built in the era of Greek-dominated Palestine culture was neither accidental nor insignificant.

God could have chosen any of history's languages to express His Word, but Greek was His chosen one. The Septuagint was the Greek translation of the Old Testament, and the New Testament's original language was Greek. It seems God handpicked Greek as the language to express Himself to all the generations from Jesus' to the end of time.

> **God could have chosen any of history's languages to express His Word, but Greek was His chosen one.**

Every language has its way of expressing love, except for those whose cultures don't include the concept of love at all in their understanding and way of life.

The Hauorani tribe of twentieth century Ecuador was one such culture. Missionary Jim Elliot and his partners, endeavoring to reach the tribe for Jesus, were faced with the task of introducing the concept of love to the Hauoranis. The tribe only knew killing and dominance as the way of relating to other people, so love was as foreign a concept to them as Christmas would be to a fish. Elliot and his four partners ultimately sacrificed their lives trying to bring the love of Christ to the tribe. Their risk of life was exactly what introduced the tribe to the idea of love, along with the missionaries' wives risking their own lives later to take the gospel to the men who had killed their husbands.

The English language has one very inadequate word to represent all the various kinds and aspects of love. It's no wonder God didn't choose English as the original language of Scripture.

As we have seen, Greek has four words for love, each representing a distinct type of love. Knowing and understanding these four words and the type of love each represents is essential to understanding Jesus, His gospel, and the life into which He invites us to live.

This book, of course, is about marital love, so marriage is its focus and purpose. But marital love is best understood by comprehending the ways Jesus loved and loves, so let's first learn from Jesus about the ways love works.

## Agape

Agape-grace is the most important of all loves. Its thread serves as the predominant one in conjunction with which the others run. Although the Greek word is simply agape, I have coined the term agape-grace because I see agape as the very same thing as grace. Grace is undeserved favor; agape is also undeserved favor. Agape and grace are more than similar, more than identical; they are the same thing by two different names.

I remember being confused by the story of Moses. He first encountered God in the burning bush on Mount Horeb; God instructed Moses to lead the Israelites back to that mountain. But Moses led the people to a mountain called Mount Sinai. Then I learned that Mount Horeb and Mount Sinai were the same mountain with two different names. It's the same with agape and grace—same concept, two different names.

I attended a Christmas party with a group of other pastors in the early 2000s and heard a devotion given by Pastor Jim Whitfield. Pastor Jimmy said "I have no problem with the virgin birth, messages from angels, instructions in dreams, miracles about shepherds or a star leading wise men across a continent to the infant Savior; what I do have trouble with is *why* He would come." Pastor Whitfield articulated the reality that the human heart can more easily digest miracles than it can comprehend the agape-grace that brought Jesus to earth and that Jesus brought to us by His coming and by everything He did and said.

Jesus came to earth to extend to humans favor we don't deserve. If you read straight through the Old Testament, you see that the Law of Moses came with consequences; if it was broken, a price was paid. Working your way through the Prophets, you read a steady string of pronouncements of judgment upon the nations. Kings and kingdoms would be upended or even destroyed because of their mistreatment of God, His instructions, other people or people groups. History, up until the advent of the Messiah, was largely the story of people getting the consequences they deserved. This was the way the one true God chose to deal with humans in the pre-Christ era. A friend of mine, Grant Covey, says the Old

Testament narrative is God showing the harm He was capable of doing. People getting what they deserved was also the mentality of the gentile world until the gospel permeated it. The Israelites' surrounding nations worshiped many different gods and were, they believed, at the mercy of the various idol-gods they served. If these gods were sufficiently reverenced, circumstances would be favorable; if not, they would not be.

Then the Christ introduced to our world something so foreign that He said it would not even fit into the world system as it currently existed; the agape-grace He introduced would destroy the vessels into which we would try to receive it, so belief in Jesus and receiving His agape-grace would necessitate our being born again, and for agape-grace to flow through us to others requires that we live life with minds constantly renewed with His truth. Jesus' old-versus-new-wineskins analogy serves to illustrate just how different and powerful agape-grace really is, and much of the work of Jesus' earthly ministry was to prepare the people of the world to receive the gift of agape-grace that He gives us.

The purpose and mission of the Son of God was to extend to humankind the undeserved favor of God. He forgave the sins of a paralyzed man and then healed him. He released an adulterous woman from the condemnation she deserved and said she was free to go. Instead of rebuking a diminutive tax collector in Jericho, He broke bread with him in his home. He delivered the daughter of a woman not even of the race called God's people and chose as His first public ambassador a Samaritan woman so sinful that the other women of the town wouldn't even allow her to join them at the town well. Over and over, Jesus offered favor to people who didn't deserve it. He diligently and thoroughly wove agape-grace as the primary thread of love to humankind. Whatever other types of love

Jesus would show His people, they would be interwoven with the thread of agape-grace.

It wasn't that Jesus spent the first part of His ministry introducing agape-grace and then moved on to another type of love; rather, He loved with agape-grace all the way to and beyond the end of His earthly life. Voluntary substitutionary death on the cross, preceded by His being ridiculed, mocked and tortured, prefaced by His being slanderously persecuted and legally prosecuted, was his final incarnate expression of agape-grace, only to be continued through His resurrection and reappearing to and communing with His followers. Agape-grace was more than a foundational layer; it was the thread that has run through the entire length of His life, ministry and legacy.

> **Jesus loved with agape-grace all the way to and beyond the end of His earthly life.**

That God the Son would go to such extreme extents to offer His favor to us who don't deserve it is the initial offering and ultimate expression of agape-grace.

## Phileo

The second Greek word for love is phileo. Often called brotherly love, it is the love close friends have for one another. In John 15 Jesus calls His disciples friends. He moved them from servant status into one of friendship. Friends are friends by the affection they have for one another, choosing to enjoy each other's presence and participation in mutual endeavors.

When I think of friendship in the Bible, my first thoughts go to David and Jonathan. Their love for each other was so strong that they each risked their safety and vulnerably confided in one another even at the possible jeopardy of each of their own royal heritage. Essential in their relationship were risk, trust, affection (They wept at the prospect of being forced apart.) and sacrifice. All these essential elements were at work in the life and ministry of Jesus, as well.

Literally putting His life on the line, Jesus gave up His very blood, breath and body so His friends could live forever. Knowing He'd be betrayed, He still trusted; foreseeing that one of His closest friends would deny even knowing Him, He still invited that friend into His most private moment on the eve of His death.

The Bible's "Love Chapter" (1 Corinthians 13) describes agape-grace. One of its characteristics is that it always trusts. This agape-grace quality is present in phileo-friendship when it's interwoven with agape-grace.

## Storge

The third love, storge, is the familial type of love. Jesus came as the Son of God, sent by the Heavenly Father, to whom Jesus submitted and whom He served. He brought His followers into the family by adoption, as brothers and sisters of His and taught us how to reverence and pray to our Heavenly Father and how to love one another as siblings.

Family is a unique unit of exclusive relationships that can be joined only by special process or invitation. Agape-grace rears its beautiful head in interwoven fashion with storge by extending the special invitation to all who would accept Jesus by faith as the Son of God who takes away the sins of the world. The invitation is to join the universe's most elite royal family. That is the storge love of God through Christ Jesus.

# Eros

The fourth Greek word for a type of love is eros, which has to do with sex and romance. Jesus is never shown in Scripture as having this type of love for someone. He didn't have a wife and that love type wasn't a part of His relationships with any woman in His life.

The way an eros type of love shows up in Jesus' relationship with humankind is by the giving of His Spirit after His death, resurrection and ascension. Eros is the physical, emotional and spiritual intimacy type of love. It's exclusively purposed for husband wife and is very dangerous without the presence of agape-grace.

When Jesus was nearing the time of His death, and again before He lifted off to ascend to the Father, He promised His followers that He would send the Holy Spirit. The Spirit, He said, had been with them, but He would soon be in them. The act of the Holy Spirit falling upon believers in Acts 2 is like what happens between husband and wife in their sex and romance life. The Spirit's outpouring was God's most intimate expression; He gave Himself to be received into the hearts of people. That's a divine model for a human married couple to follow in giving of themselves to each other in the most intimate way.

For this most intimate divine expression to humans to occur, a prerequisite had to be met: Jesus had to die. It was expedient, He told the disciples, that He go away, so the promised Holy Spirit could come. Whereas Jesus had been with them performing miracles and teaching them precious truths, the Holy Spirit would continue His work in and through believers. For the intimate work of God to be carried out in people, the Son had to die and join the Father in Heaven. Before Jesus could practice His version of eros, He had to carry out the final foundational act of agape-grace, literally dying for His bride.

Having God abide within us by His Spirit is the closest possible relationship for us with Him. This was Jesus' ultimate goal and plan for us. That's how we would have any semblance of His promise of our doing even greater things than He did (because I go to the Father, He added). Jesus' love for us would be delivered through His eventual death, which led to His resurrection, ascension and giving of the Spirit.

The focus in this chapter is the life of Jesus. But as we move on later pages into applications to marital love, please keep in mind, concerning eros, these three examples of God:

1. Jesus died for, among other purposes, the selfless purpose of opening the pathway for the Holy Spirit to be sent into our hearts.

2. God gives believers His Spirit, not only for the joy of His experiencing us, but, more importantly to Him, for our joy of experiencing Him.

3. God never uses the promise of giving His Spirit to coerce us into performance of certain behavior but gives freely to all who are His by faith in Christ.

Jesus interwove the threads of love in His life and ministry that we believers may do the same in our lives and ministries, including our marriages.

# 6

# The Four Greek Loves in Marriage

Jesus had died, arisen, ascended, and released the promised Holy Spirit. The church had been birthed in Jerusalem and branched out to the greater Jewish area and Samaria. The apostles had taken the gospel to regions and cities around the Mediterranean Sea where the church continued to flourish. Paul established many local churches and wrote follow-up letters to them, instructing each congregation about topics specific to their needs.

Ephesus was a major Roman city well known for its idolatry. The Temple of Artemis was there as a constant reminder of the pagan belief system official to the city. Artemis was a goddess her worshippers believed to have come from Zeus' extramarital affair and whose standards for marriage were diabolically different from the gospel's.

The church birthed from the ministry of Paul also involved the husband-wife team of Aquilla and Priscilla. In the pagan culture and the physical Temple of Artemis, the Ephesian church faced a constant afront to the Christian model of marriage.

It is in the epistle of Paul to this congregation that we find what is arguably the most essential scriptural passage on marriage. Ephesians 5:22-26 reveals what God desires for the husband and for the wife. The husband is to follow the example set by the Lord Jesus of sacrificial love for His bride, the church, while the wife is to live as the church was purposed to live, in submission to her groom.

Readers of that passage who are part of a more gender-equal culture, like ours, often have problems digesting these verses and the idea that the wife is the spouse who is to do the submitting while the husband is likened to the Lord. In response to this difficulty, I offer three points:

**Christ was supremely submissive.**
There never has been a person who submitted themselves more than did the Son of God. Deserving to be worshiped, He quietly accepted the mistreatment of Jewish and Roman leaders. Perfect and without sin, He took the punishment His bride, the church, deserved so that she could go free and have abundant life.

**Loving leadership involves extensive submission.**
A husband with the idea that the wife does the submitting while he does the leading understands neither leadership, love, nor marriage. Effective leadership includes setting examples for those they lead, and the power of exemplifying humility and submission is greater than many realize. Leadership without humility is arrogant domineering, which does nothing but ruin a marriage.

**Agape love inherently puts the welfare of others before self.**
The entire 1 Corinthians 13 description of agape places its focus on the object (recipient) of love rather than the one expressing it.

This section, which includes the next four chapters, applies the four Greek loves specifically to marriage. Remember that the fabric of marital love will consist of all four, each in its purpose and measure, with agape being more prevalent than phileo, storge and eros, combined. But also keep in mind that marriage is the only relationship that includes all four, and that each is uniquely essential to a marriage.

Returning to the idea of the husband and wife's respective roles in marriage, my wife, Sharlene, and I were in a marriage class at our church back in the nineties. Sharlene shared with me that she was understanding submission like she hadn't before. What opened her eyes, and mine as well, was one truth. The matter was mainly between the wife and God. The Lord never tells the husband to help his wife submit or hold her accountable in her submissive wife life. She answers to God about it, not her husband. In fact, the husband has his hands full with all the submitting that comes along with his responsibility to love his wife as Christ loves the church.

Sharlene's revelation about submission inspired me to invite her opinion about how I could be a better husband. In my arrogance, I expected her to answer that I was doing everything well with no room for improvement. But her answer humbled me. "I wish you were more the spiritual leader of our family," she said in a soft, kind way. At first, it threw me for a loop because I was a pastor on staff at our church in charge of several ministries; I *was* a spiritual leader. But as I thought about it, and we talked, I realized I had been taking my spiritual leader hat off before walking into our home after work every night.

Look at what happened in that scenario. My wife, with a submissive heart, offered tender advice I solicited, and it led to my being a better leader in our marriage and family. I had to travel through submission, myself, on my way to improving my leadership. God's Word can always be trusted and obeyed. This is an example of what always happens when we do comply with His Word: we're blessed by an increase of abundance of life.

> *Therefore, just as the church is subject to Christ, so let the wives be to their own husbands in everything. Husbands, love your wives, just as Christ also loved the church and gave Himself for her* (Ephesians 5:24-25 NKJV).

# 7

# Agape Love in Marriage

Since agape is the most important love—the most important of all factors, for that matter—in marriage, it's worth the time it takes to master it.

To give a succinct definition for agape, I would offer: *love given with nothing required in return from the recipient.*

Scripture is replete with expressions of agape love. The most direct passages are 1 Corinthians 13 and 1 John 4. The teachings of Jesus in the Gospels give clear vision for application, as do the grace expoundings of the epistle writers of the New Testament. In the Old Testament narrative of God's treatment of humankind, praise of God's acts of grace in the Psalms and prophecies of His planned offerings of grace all combine with the New Testament material to provide a complete understanding of God's love, grace, and gospel.

Agape took on its meaning as Jesus and the New Testament writers used it. This type of love didn't exist outside of God and His grace, certainly not among the Greeks, so God used the word agape to represent His idea of loving us. In other words, it was the writers of Scripture who took agape through its quick etymological process

> **Agape took on its meaning as Jesus and the New Testament writers used it.**

and crafted it pronto into the word we know it to be today.

Agape, in my opinion, is the same as grace. Agape and grace aren't similar, or even identical; they are the same thing with two different names.

To help explain that, let me give you an example. I remember discovering that Mount Horeb, where Moses encountered God in the burning bush, and Mount Sinai were two different names for the same mountain. Prior to learning that, I had been confused that God instructed Moses to return with the Israelites to Mount Horeb only to read that Moses led the people to Mount Sinai. Understanding that Moses was obedient and that the mountain had two names cleared things up for me. Perhaps it will be as helpful for us to realize that grace and agape are two names for the same thing: God's unmerited favor.

It's interesting (to a word geek like me, at least) that the English *grace* translates from the Greek *charis*; some older English Bible versions use the word "charity," an English word for love centuries ago, for agape. Charis and charity are too similar to go unnoticed. So, by either mere coincidence or some inexplicable poetic occurrence agape love and grace seem destined to be two different words expressing God's loving grace.

Now let's apply the description of 1 Corinthians 13, phrase by phrase, to marriage.

**Without love…**

Paul is transitioning, , from the subject of gifts of the Holy Spirit and how and why they should function in a body of Christian worshippers. Their purpose, in a nutshell, is to edify said body. He begins the thirteenth chapter by adding a factor, agape-love, in the equation. Without agape, Paul emphasizes, all these gifts, including the most valuable as well as the most coveted, are worthless. Agape gives these gifts value and adds the wonderful benefit of bringing unity to the brothers and sisters in Christ.

Agape carries the same purpose in its role in a marriage; it unifies. As we make our way through 1 Corinthian's thirteenth chapter and agape's descriptive phrases, we see progressively with each quality more clearly how agape unifies husband and wife.

And, like the family of believers, it matters little what strengths and gifts the two spouses each bring into the marriage, unless they embrace agape-love for one another. We could substitute Paul's words in verses 1 thru 3 with: though a husband speaks with the greatest charm and moves Heaven with his eloquence, though the wife is so intuitive that she can predict the couples' future, and though both spouses are so generous and thoughtful that they feed and clothe all the needy in their community, and though this husband and wife are so sacrificial that they would allow their very bodies to be sacrificed, if they do not have agape-love for each other, they will not have a good marriage.

I'm a huge basketball fan; over the years I've seen teams with so many great players that their success was a given. Stacked with a starting five that would all be in the top ten players in the league, the potential points to nothing short of a championship. Yet, somehow, their season doesn't turn out very successful. There's something they're missing. It isn't talent, individual skills, even playmaking and passing skills, factors one would assume would guarantee the team gelling to maximize all their other skills and defeating any other team. The team could even have a coach wise enough to manage personalities and coach them to victories. But there's something missing, something nobody can figure out. The team falls far short of expectations. They don't win the championship; they don't even make it to the championship.

Likewise, a married couple can have high expectations because of their strengths as a couple; maybe the high expectations are theirs, or maybe those outside their marriage hold those expectations, or maybe it's both. But then the couple runs into major problems, problems they're ill equipped to handle because they catch them by surprise.

My wife and I have counseled many couples who were dealing with problems in their relationship they couldn't seem to fix; with no exceptions, they've all been very frustrated. Then, at some point, we put our finger on the problem: each of them was looking at their spouse's issue as the problem. Once we can get them to each look at their own issue and accept responsibility, themselves, they can start moving in the direction of the solution.

It's remarkable. The moment one or both spouses begin looking at their responsibility instead of the other's, it's like a light has switched on and the room is no longer dark. It's such a satisfying feeling for counselors and married couples when they make that critical adjustment. And it all comes down to agape love. Once they enact agape toward each other, victory is soon—often immediately—achieved.

> **Having patience in marriage means one spouse never gives up on the other spouse.**

**Love Is Patient.**

Having patience in marriage means one spouse never gives up on the other spouse. James 1 tells us how patience is built, tested, and utilized. James says it's the trials testing our faith that produce patience. So, we can expect in the endeavor of gaining patience, to have troubles so fiery that they push the limits of our faith. At that point, don't withdraw from the process, James says, but let patience be fully developed. Finally, he reveals that patience, once gained, will assure our completeness. It will be the thing—a never-give-up factor—that takes us through any storm or attack that comes against us.

This tells us that our marriages will never end as long as the spouses are alive so we should not give up on each other. And we can see marriage as a breeding ground for the faith that will carry each of us all the way through to the end, taking us into eternity with God. Marriage is worth fighting for, and agape's first named quality of being patient is needed more than anything else in the fight.

In the early 1800s, boxing was a different sport than we know it to be today. It was called pugilism and was much more brutal and violent; fighters didn't wear gloves and were allowed to grapple as well as strike. There were no weight classes, no maximum number of rounds, no TKOs or decisions made by judges. Fights were fought until one of the competitors was unable to continue.

One such fight was held in England between John Rutledge and James Sax. Sax outweighed Rutledge by nearly fifty pounds and was far more skilled and experienced. The fight began with a right hook by Sax that sent Rutledge to the canvas; after the fight, Rutledge told newspaper reporters that the first punch knocked the breath out of him, and it felt like every bone he had was rattled. After the first round, Rutledge told his trainer he couldn't go on, but the trainer convinced him to go out for one more round.

In round two, Rutledge took a terrible beating that broke his nose and cracked several ribs. Rutledge again told his manager he couldn't continue, but again his trainer convinced him to fight just one more round.

Rounds three, four, and five saw Sax knock Rutledge down

twice in each round. The battered fighter was almost unable to get to his feet after each knockdown. Rutledge argued to not continue each time he came to his corner, but his persistent trainer persuaded him to fight the next round. This went on for twenty-seven rounds. After twenty-seven rounds of being brutally assaulted, Rutledge came to the end of himself. With broken ribs, a broken nose, jaw, and eye socket, he couldn't continue, and his trainer agreed.

But when the bell rang to begin round twenty-eight, John stood up, not to fight but to leave the ring; however, as soon as Rutledge stood, the referee waved his arms and shouted, "This fight is over!"

John and his trainer were both surprised, neither having notified the referee of Rutledge's inability to continue. At that moment, the referee pointed to the opponent's corner and shouted, "Mr. Sax is unable to continue! Mr. Rutledge is the winner!" (This story is completely fictitious, created to illustrate the power of not quitting, because some marriages may require this kind of patience.)

The enemy of our marriages—the devil—is the same as the enemy of our souls and our God. He's a deceiving accuser with seemingly relentless attacks, but God's Word, in James 4, promises us that he will flee from us if we resist him. It may take much patience and perseverance, but he will flee. Like John Rutledge, we may be ready to throw in the towel, but if we just continue to resist, we'll have an often-surprising victory. Agape love is patient, which sometimes means fighting the enemy for our spouse and marriage.

The stronger the urge to give up, the more patience is required. This applies to marriage as much as anything else. Never giving up on our spouse or our marriage is sometimes the very thing that will bring marital success.

**Love Is Kind.**

If there's a place where we need kindness, it's when we come home to our spouse. Getting back home often seems like an escape from an unkind world where we long for the lovingkindness of our spouse's arms. To actually find such kindness from the person we depend on most is supremely satisfying; to not find it must be the utmost in disappointment.

When I think of kindness, synonyms come to mind, like tenderness, care, comfort, generosity, and responsiveness. I found these qualities waiting for me when I returned home from the hospital after a major stroke. Sharlene, having never left my bedside during my month-long hospital stay, doted on me at every opportunity at home, and where opportunity didn't exist, she created it.

Every night for months Sharlene came around to my side of our bed and tucked me in after taking and recording my vitals. She cooked every meal, took care of every need I had, and staved off my normal responsibilities;. Though it taxed her daily, she seemed to take pleasure in doing it all.

Still, I would often feel sorry for her. Several times I said something to the effect of, "I'm sorry. I know this isn't how we dreamed our lives would turn out. I'm sorry you're stuck taking care of me like this." Every time—every time!—her response was, "I'm doing exactly what I want to do."

Kindness can be positively overwhelming when it comes from your spouse. I can't prevent tears even now (four years later) as I write this recounting.

> Kindness can be positively overwhelming when it comes from your spouse.

**Love Does Not Envy.**

I have to confess that, though I had never previously experienced envy toward my wife, I have faced this temptation in the grandparent stage of our lives as I've seen our grandkids sometimes give the greater attention to Lolli (Sharlene). I'm pleased to say I've never given in to that temptation; God has given me the strength and made it somehow easy for me. But envy has, on those occasions when the grands would, upon entering our home, run past me (G Pop) without a glance, yelling "Lolli!" How do I explain my never surrendering to the temptation? It may be that God used the obvious realization that Lolli deserves the attention to shield me from taking on envy toward my wife; or perhaps it's just the agape love that God has placed in my heart for Sharlene. Regardless of how He's done it, He has kept me from falling victim to envy's draw and allowed me to continue in agape love toward my spouse. Thank God!

A common scenario where envy exists in marriage is when one spouse becomes jealous of the other's career situation. For example, one spouse resents that the other gets to thrive in a career while they're "stuck" with the kids, or the one spouse seems more successful in their field than the other does in theirs; one spouse has active friendships while the other for some reason doesn't; one spouse's family behaves better than the other's; one's more skilled in some area than the other; one's metabolism makes weight control easier or growing muscle less laborious. The scenarios can go on and on. The important thing is to choose agape love, the love that places no requirements on the receiver and especially that they not one-up them in some way. Agape love is being okay with being disadvantaged in some way.

**Love Does Not Boast.**

For the spouse that happens to find themselves in an advantaged position compared to their spouse, how do they handle it? It isn't by boasting about it. Could Lolli flaunt the attention she gets from the grands? Yes, but agape love, to which she's committed, shields her heart from such ugliness.

You can see how agape love, as it excludes envy and boasting, is unifying for a married couple.

**Love Is Not Proud.**

To be proud is to think of oneself more highly than they are. This automatically places others, including the spouse and even God, lower than they really are. This would obviously be a problem in any relationship. In truth, a relationship infected with pride is bound for destruction, a truth we infer from Proverbs.

Pride throws things out of kilter, and places things out of order. One of the biblical Greek words translated *world* in English is *kosmos*, which is a near transliteration to *cosmos* in our language. The word means *order*. We use it to refer to the systematic arrangement of the stellar bodies in the universe. The New Testament uses the word to differentiate between the contrasting kingdoms of heaven and hell, hell being the system headed by Satan that leaves God out (Rev. Dr. Tony Evans' definition). The heavenly kingdom is ordered by God's will with Him as its king. Hell is ordered—or disordered—by Satan, its king and god (called the god of this age in 2 Corinthians 4:4). Hell was formed from Satan's prideful rebellion against God and is now a deformed system of evil whose future is destruction. All that disorder and doom resulted from pride, Satan having the idea that he is higher than he is and that, therefore, God and His holy angels are lower than they are.

The marriage infected by pride will have a similar fate, its only hope being repentance with humility. With pride, order will be compromised, God's design perverted, and two people very disappointed in their marriage. Pride manifested in a marriage will be domination, manipulation, entitlement, unfaithfulness, and mistreatment of every variety. Yet all this can be averted by prideless agape love.

## Love Is Not Self-Seeking.

What quality draws two together with each one putting the other before themselves? Talk about a unifying quality! I've seen this over and over in my marriage, when both Sharlene and I choose a humbler position that the other may be exalted. I'm not sure anything draws us together more powerfully than the experience of non-self-seeking.

## Love Is Not Easily Angered.

Slow to anger is a recognizable scriptural calling to serious Jesus followers. The Christian marriage will recognize and accept that call.

The last major argument Sharlene and I had was in the year 2000. We disagreed so strongly about something that I left for the night, drove to a hotel, and spent the night alone. Seething, I didn't sleep a wink; neither, I found out later, did Sharlene. I drove home the next morning, parked the car, and met Sharlene outside the back door as she had been watching for my return. We fell on each other's neck, embraced nearly without end, and apologized profusely, both of us relieved that our conflict was over.

Sharlene and I have both admitted, as we've assessed that situation over the years since, the reason that was the finale of our huge argument life was that we both endured such pain from our angry treatment of one another that we didn't want to ever experience it again.

By this experience and some others, I've learned that agape love and its qualities can be developed. While agape does come from God, He also gives us the wisdom and strength to progress in our wielding of it.

## Love Keeps No Record of Wrongs.

This one trait of agape love connects it, like super glue, to grace. Grace is favor that's unmerited. Agape love doesn't include keeping track of demerits. Lack of merit is a nonfactor, as if it doesn't exist. In fact, it doesn't. Wrongs of one spouse toward another bounce off like BB pellets hitting an army tank when the agape-loving spouse has predetermined that wrongs will be of no effect. They are built to resist offense to their spouse. This is what Christ the Groom has done for His bride, and spouses in Christ-centered marriage will follow suit.

## Love Does Not Delight in Evil
## but Rejoices with the Truth.

The agape-loving spouse is elated when their spouse receives a just reward. No matter how much they'd relish receiving such a blessing themselves, they find it most fulfilling that the other person rightly enjoys the good blessing. This quality seems a close sibling to the one of not envying.

## Love always protects.

Agape love originates with Almighty God, who has the power to protect the objects of His love from any threat at any time. As we take on the agape we've received from Him and apply it to objects of our own, we have to recognize our limited ability to protect. What doesn't have to be limited, though, are the protective intentions we hold in our hearts and the actions that naturally exude from there.

We need protection in every aspect of our lives, so agape-protection is more than shielding from physical harm. Spouses need their counterpart's emotional protection, protection of their name and reputation, financial protection, protection of their kids, parents, and all they love. The attitude of protection is spring fed by spousal agape love. From that natural spring flows a passion to do everything possible to make their spouse safe and healthy in every sense.

I was forty-five years old when, one morning, I had a bout with vertigo. Vertigo was a new experience for me, and even though we'd heard of others having it, Sharlene and I knew very little about it. After lying on the couch a couple hours, unable to turn my head without becoming nauseated, I asked Sharlene to research this condition to see how serious it was. Of course, she found an array of possible causes and prognoses, one of which was that vertigo could possibly be linked to cancer. Sharlene decided to get me up and get me to a doctor. As I was walking down the hallway to go out the front door, our kids were watching me holding on to furniture and the wall to keep my balance; they all looked worried.

I began to imagine that I could have cancer and could be in my last days on the earth with my family. As I got into the passenger seat of our Suburban, I teared up and said to Sharlene in the driver seat, "What if the Lord is taking me home soon?" Without hesitation Sharlene responded with absolute certainty, "That's not gonna happen!" as she drove onto the street, commanding the large SUV with great authority. I knew as the words left her mouth that they were true. Sharlene is someone with strong faith and can be very determined, so I had no doubt that God would answer her prayer and protect her husband from any serious harm. What a comforting feeling to know that my spouse was using every ounce of the faith and determination she had to protect me.

**Love Always Trusts.**

I've heard comments like, "forgiveness and trust are two different things," "I love him, but I'll never be able to trust him again," and, "God doesn't expect us to trust someone who's not trustworthy." According to Paul's second letter to the Corinthian church, those sentiments are just that—sentiments only. The Holy Spirit makes it clear here that agape love offers trust without regard to what the recipient will do with it.

> The Holy Spirit makes it clear that agape love offers trust without regard to what the recipient will do with it.

Admittedly, this characteristic of love is not only surprising but counterintuitive. What sense does it make for a spouse to open themselves up to more physical abuse after dozens of beatings? Why should an exasperated spouse give access to an updated bank account to the recovering addict spouse who just relapsed and spent every dime they had and maxed out their credit cards? In what world is it advisable to allow a verbally abusive spouse to move back in while their spouse's wounds are just beginning to heal? Let me say, clearly that strong measures should be taken to lower— ideally, eliminate—the likelihood of continued havoc in these scenarios, but agape love would dictate that we find a path that will lead us to trust again.

Then I think about how God has trusted me. My track record for money management is less than stellar, but He still provides for all my financial needs, regularly placing more money than I deserve, or even need, in my hands. He's given me nearly endless opportunities despite my history of squandering so many chances to succeed. I had been neither a good son nor sibling, but He enriched my life with the best wife and kids, six of them, and, to date, eight wonderful grandchildren, trusting me with increase in family relationships.

And when I consider my trusting of God, how I've consistently come up short in trusting His hand, His heart, and His Word, I'm tempted to be ashamed. But the comparison is apparent. God has placed more trust in me, the supremely untrustworthy, than I have in Him, even though He's completely trustworthy. So, agape love trusts, even if it's the trustworthy trusting the unreliable.

And lest we be tempted to see this single statement, *love always trusts*, as unsupported by Scripture as a whole, we may recall from the Messiah: *turn the other cheek…walk with him two miles…bring the best robe, shoes, and the ring…* Trusting is a strong theme from the Bible's opening pages to its closing ones. Should we trust God? Yes. But we also need to give that trust to those with failed attempts at earning trust. Why else would God trust the descendants of Noah when his ancestors had grieved Him so? Why would he issue a string of opportunities to people like Samson, Saul, and the kings of Israel?

It's in the context of our human world that agape love stands out so antithetically, yet it's our world into which He's ushered in His grace, His kingdom, His gospel.

Think about how God knows exactly what we're going to do with a resource He places into our hands, yet He entrusts it to us even when He knows we'll mismanage it. Regarding giving, many people operate with the practice of only giving to responsible recipients. I consider a recipient's history and likelihood of responsible resource management when making giving decisions, but we shouldn't require a perfect track record of a recipient. Following God's example of generosity means we'll sometimes give to people who won't manage our gift well. Jesus trusted, knowing the trusted weren't trustworthy, and we may trust others, including our spouses, and at times be disappointed. Trusting is part of being a spouse, and so is sometimes being disappointed.

## Love Always Hopes.

Here's another great surprise—God pours His hope upon us. His agape love hopes in us despite our lack of promise. Of all the beings to hope in, why would He choose us?

Sports fans may be the closest parallel to this aspect of God's love. Some cities somehow believe year after year that their team will win the Super Bowl, the World Series, or the Stanley Cup but their team loses season after season. They're so committed, so undeterred in their belief in their team that they genuinely expect this to be "the year." Loyalty defies logic in these cases.

But with God, we aren't dealing with illogical thinking; He knows exactly what the future holds and how things will turn out. So how can agape love always hope?

I believe the secret lies in the interpretation of success. God is certain we'll succeed, but then we fail. Or do we? Agape love knows how to see the victories in what hatred or despisal cannot.

I used to watch *The Dean Smith Show* on Sunday mornings when I was a teenager. A diehard Tarheels basketball fan, I relished the insider comments of the legendary coach as he reviewed game film with the viewers. It struck me that this genius coach who demanded excellence from his players would often point out the minor points of success his team had had. They lost the game but outrebounded the opponent. They didn't score well, but their shot selection was good. A certain player had made improvement since earlier in the season in the area of turnovers. It was refreshing to watch this great winner compliment his team, especially in the wake of a loss.

God's hope in us must have to do with His ability to see our hidden successes through His lens of agape love. It's through this same lens that spouses must view one another. I'm one of those people who has a spouse who believes in me unconditionally. Sharlene always believes I can meet whatever challenge lies before me. When I'm deciding whether to embark upon or continue in something difficult, she always encourages me to go for it. She's never surprised when I succeed, and when I fail, she's quick to point out my smaller victories—what I did accomplish or do well within the context of coming up short overall.

**From the standpoint of a husband in whom his wife always finds hope, I can tell you that it is immeasurably strengthening.**

I was the lead pastor of Grace Harbor Church for ten years, a church we planted and loved. When I sensed God leading me to step down and take on a different ministry focus—writing—I found myself disappointed as I looked back on our Grace Harbor experience. I saw the endeavor as a fail-ure, never having built the church to large numbers. But Sharlene disagreed; when I would lament GHC as a failure, she would remind me of the people we led to

Christ, the friends we gained, and the seeds we sowed that are continuing to bear fruit.

From the standpoint of a husband in whom his wife always finds hope, I can tell you that it is immeasurably strengthening.

**Love Always Perseveres.**

Here we are, having come full circle. Paul began with the statement, *love is patient*; now, at the end of his description of agape love, he reiterates the idea, just with different words. Agape love is unending—enduring any circumstances and never giving up, no matter what, on its object.

For the married couple, unfaithfulness on the part of one party is the only out for the other, but even adultery doesn't necessarily terminate agape love. I've known several couples that continued their marriages after adultery on the part of one spouse; some of them are still married, but one of those marriages soon ended because the offended spouse was unable to continue in complete forgiveness. I've also known offended spouses to be willing to continue the marriage while the adulterer spouse was not. This isn't surprising when you consider the adulterous spouse's heart had already turned away while the faithful one's never had, having been none the wiser to their spouse's unfaithfulness. While it's understandably extremely difficult for a couple to overcome adultery, the offended spouse having every right to exercise their freedom, nothing says they must.

Short of unfaithfulness, one's imminent danger from the other, or death, though, nothing should bring a marriage to a close. Agape love doesn't expire; it always perseveres. This is the importance of agape love in marriage; it's the best precluder of divorce. And an ended marriage doesn't close the door on agape. Most of us know divorced couples with an amicable relationship, whether for the sake of co-parenting or because the former spouses simply don't abhor each other. Remember, agape's scope includes everyone, even our enemies, which for some includes exes.

**Love Never Fails.**

This is the final descriptive of agape in the "love chapter." Again, agape is proclaimed to be invincible. If you're looking to not only divorce-proof your marriage but to guarantee its success by any godly standard, walk in agape love for each other. By the Word of God, you will never fail.

Let's now turn our attention to the other love chapter, 1 John 4. I see two major ideas about agape in this fourth chapter of 1 John. Agape love originates with God, and because we receive agape we can and must give agape love.

For spouses, this means that, for a marriage to have agape love, it must include God. People can try to love with agape love, but the very best they'll do without faith in Jesus, the only way to God, is an inconsistent, fragmented, one day on and three days off kind of selfless love.

> **It's the Holy Spirit dwelling in the hearts of the two Jesus-following spouses that actually produces agape love.**

So there we have it—the single most important ingredient for marriage—that Jesus Christ be given the throne of the marriage, both spouses subjecting individually and as a couple to the marriage plan of God. This inevitably means both spouses are trusting Jesus for their eternal salvation and for every part of life on earth. The married couple fully surrendered to Jesus is perfectly positioned for the best possible marriage because both those spouses have the Holy Spirit, agape love dwelling naturally and constantly inside their hearts.

It's the Holy Spirit dwelling in the hearts of the two Jesus-following spouses that actually produces agape love. Agape love is the first fruit produced by the Spirit, as we read in Galatians 5:22.

## Intensity of Agape Love

Intensity is a factor for all the types of love in marriage. It's possible to go through the motions of loving with agape without it coming powerfully from your heart's desires. I know this because I've been guilty of it. At times in my marriage I've committed to show Sharlene all the characteristics of agape love when it had more to do with obeying the letter of love's law than it did with the woman for whom it was intended. God soon convicted me and taught me more about real agape love.

In 2 Kings 13 is the story of Elisha and King Jehoash. The king is visiting the prophet Elisha who is on his deathbed. Elisha knows that the king is threatened by the Aramean army and instructs him to shoot an arrow out of the bedroom window and then beat the ground with the remaining arrows. The king beats the ground, but Elisha gets upset at the number—only three—times he hit the ground, admonishing him for not striking "five or six times." Had he struck with more zeal, his victory over the Arameans would've been more complete.

I always had trouble with that story. How could the prophet be upset when the king obeyed his instructions? If he was expected to do more, why wasn't it made clear to begin with?

Finally, I realized (with God's help) that the point is to be passionate for the things of God. Passion is fiery desire, and it's with such passion that God loves us. If God's agape love is highly passionate, so should ours be toward our spouse. To increase our passion and desire, remember the three eds:

### Yielded
Although the Son of God was sent to earth with a specific assignment—to save us from our sin by sacrificing His life—on the eve of the appointed time for the sacrifice, His desire was that the Father might change the plan. As Jesus knelt, blood seeping through His skin in His anxious state, He uttered the ultimate prayer of surrender, *Nevertheless, not My will but Yours be done.* The Messiah demonstrated for us the course of action when our desires don't match up with God's: yield.

### Delighted
In Psalms 37:4 David recorded the formula for both developing desires and having them met. That formula is simply to put your delight in the Lord; when we do that, David reasoned, God will give to us what our hearts desire. Pertaining to marriage, I've learned that when I ruminate on my wife's good qualities, I become more delighted by her and desiring of her. This adds fuel to the fire of agape love for my spouse, making it more like the passionate kind that God has for us.

> I've learned that when I ruminate on my wife's good qualities, I become more delighted by her and desiring of her.

### Filled
I've learned that I cannot drink alcohol. My history of drinking has proven that I have trouble stopping short of excess, so I've committed to be a teetotaler. Therefore, I don't have to worry

about the first half of Ephesians 5:18, "Do not get drunk on wine, which leads to debauchery. Instead, be filled with the Spirit." What I do fill myself with, however, requires intentionality on my part—"but be filled with the Spirit," as the balance of the verse goes. When we spend time in fellowship with the Spirit He increases, and we decrease. As this happens, it's natural that our desires give way to the Spirit's, fueling our passion to love with the Spirit's agape love. So, key to having a passionate agape love for our spouse is to be filled with the Spirit. A spouse devoid of God's Spirit will be no agape-lover. Drawing ourselves close to God, making the sacrifice of time and attention to do so is critical if we're to have intense agape love.

> Key to having a passionate agape love for our spouse is to be filled with the Spirit.

# 8

# Phileo Love in Marriage

Phileo is defined by *Strong's* as the love between friends. Its more popular definition is brotherly love (the city of Philadelphia is called the city of brotherly love). That understanding probably comes from Romans 12:10, which, using the Greek phileo, admonishes believers to love one another with brotherly love. What Paul meant to get across in that verse is that we should love our friends (brothers and sisters in Christ) in the same way we love our natural siblings.

When I was seven years old, I had three sisters. My mom was expecting my fourth sibling, but in those days, you didn't know the gender until the baby was born. Tired of being outnumbered, I was desperate for a brother; I even told my parents that if this child wasn't a boy, I was going to run away from home. I'm sure they weren't concerned that I'd have the courage to leave or how far I'd get if I did, but they knew my seven-year-old heart was serious about having a brother. Looking back, I know now that I was always close friends with my sisters, although I didn't realize it at the time. But I wanted a brother; in my mind, there was something missing in my life, and I just knew a little brother would fill the void.

When the baby was born, it was a boy. My parents gave me the good news; then they gave me another gift, the privilege of naming my little brother. Certainly, they reserved veto power, should I suggest something ridiculous, but all they said to me was that, since having a brother was so important to me, I could choose his name.

After giving it some thought, I settled on the name Jonathan. Having recently learned in Sunday school what a close friendship David had with Jonathan and wanting that kind of close friendship with my brother, that had to be his name. My parents concurred. My brother, Jonathan, and I have always been close. When I went off to college and became homesick, it was Jonathan whom I missed most. Some nights I lay in my dorm room bed with tears as I processed the emotions that came with moving into this new chapter of my life.

David and Jonathan exemplify phileo love as well as any we can find. They each made significant sacrifice for the other—David pledged to always bless Jonathan and his family, a pledge he kept throughout his life, and Jonathan relinquished to David any hold he might possibly have had on the throne of Israel.

From another of Paul's writings, 1 Corinthians 16:22, we see that we are to love Jesus, Himself, as if He is our brother. And it's because He is the firstborn among all us brothers and sisters brought into God's family through adoption.

Throughout my elementary, middle, and high school years, I had a string of close friends, male classmates with common interests. My understanding of friendship was just that—people of the same gender with common interests who hit it off in a special way.

In elementary school, my best friend was Jim. My mom taught me one day that God wants to be our friend, and we should think of Him as such. I took that to heart, spending several weeks talking to God and calling Him Jim. I knew that God knew my heart and took my temporary alias for Him with joy as I grew closer to Him in the process.

It never crossed my mind that spouses would be friends. The married couples I saw up close, my parents and paternal grandparents, didn't display much friendship in their relationships. I thought my eventual marriage would be mostly about sex and romance with, perhaps, some parenting added to the mix along with working with my wife to lead our household.

One of the most pleasant surprises I found in my early marriage was the close, strong friendship Sharlene and I had. We both genuinely enjoyed each other. We played tennis and basketball together, sang together, read many of the same books, served in our church together, and generally loved being together, accomplishing things, talking, and having fun together. Our friendship wasn't something we gave much thought to; it just occurred organically as we went about our life together. It developed from the time we began our dating relationship and was strong and healthy by the time we married. Though we weren't fully aware of it at the time, it was our love for each other as friends that got us past our early marriage conflicts. Friendship was the strongest part of our marriage relationship, phileo the strongest of the four loves connecting us. We didn't realize that at first, but over time we came to appreciate our friendship and generally gave it priority over other friendships and any of the other love types we had for one another. Unfamiliar with agape love in those days, phileo was the priority love type for both of us. It happened this way pretty naturally, for the most part. From an organic standpoint—the natural growth of something without much effort or interference—phileo was the strongest of the loves in our marriage.

But even that strongest love began to subside, much to our surprise, as storge, by necessity, pulled out front during our early parenting years. Parenting was the focus of most of our time, energy, and resources. But we soon realized our friendship was taking a hit.

That realization began on our sixth wedding anniversary. From the beginning of our marriage, we had gone every year on an overnight trip, some years as long as ten days and nights away, to celebrate our anniversary. This sixth year, we checked into the hotel, got up to our room, settled in, and sat down. Our attempts to have simple conversation, we noticed, were surprisingly laborious, which was awkward. Somewhat alarmed, we both acknowledged the problem and quickly detected the root cause. All we had in common, all there was for us to talk about, the thing that consumed us and snuffed out all other parts of our marriage, was parenting the kids. At that point, Sharlene was pregnant with Kristin, our third child, and our first two, Tres and Nate, were ages four and two. As important a priority as parenting was, we knew parenting would one day subside, and we'd be left with an empty nest and whatever marriage investment we'd made over the years.

So then and there, we made a pact. We wouldn't allow anything, even our all-important parenting life to trump investment in our marriage. We've kept the pact over the years, and still now we both agree that our friendship is the strongest part of our marriage, and our marriage the most important relationship in either of our lives.

Phileo being the Greek love friends have for each other, it can be very intimate, but not sexual, except in marriage, for those committed to a biblical lifestyle. Friendship can cross over into any type of relationship, including family or any type of partnership.

I've noticed a trend of people recognizing their spouse as their best friend. I think that's a wonderful direction for marriages to take, making our spouse our closest friend.

However, I did once see that someone wrote on social media, "Twenty years ago I asked my high school sweetheart, my best friend, and the love of my life, to marry me. Unfortunately, all three said no, but everything turned out pretty good; happy anniversary [wife]."

To organize the study of love between friends, I use P-H-I-L-E-O as an acrostic. A good friend can show love to their friend in these ways: Presence, Helping, Intercession, Lifting, Empathy, and Offering.

**Presence**

Good friends are present and available for each other. The story of Job follows the great loss Job experienced and his response to that loss. Three of his friends showed up to help. For several days Job's friends said nothing; they just sat with him.

> Good friends are present and available for each other.

Eventually, Job's friends broke their silence. The writer doesn't include any commentary, only narrative, but I feel safe in saying that Job preferred their silent presence over their words. When they began speaking, they proved the opposite of helpful. They were accusatory and inconsiderate of their friend who had just lost virtually all his substantial wealth along with his ten children.

The only family member who remained after the onslaught of destruction upon Job was his wife. However, she provided what may be the worst example in history of how a spouse should respond to their spouse's troubles. She foolishly advised him to curse God and die. (In her counsel, she could have at least included repentance before dying.) Admittedly, unlike Job's other friends, his wife shared directly in the loss. Nevertheless, hers is not a model anyone would want their spouse to follow. Like Job's visiting friends, his wife's silence would've been preferred over her advice.

Presence is a simple provision to make if we are just willing to put everything on pause for our friend. It requires no advice or action other than just being with them and making mental notes as we observe them in their time of trouble.

Our son Nate had asthma as a child. Several times in his years as a small child, he had to be hospitalized. During one hospitalization, Nate, who was three years old, was apprehensive about any hospital staff entering the room. Upon the entry of any person into his room, Nate would say, "Mom, I love you. Dad, I love you. Mom...Dad..." Sharlene and I loved hearing those words, even though we knew they just meant, "Mom, Dad, I'm afraid, and I need you here with me." Our presence meant safety and protection to him in those moments.

As the Israelites readied themselves to move forward after the death of Moses to follow Joshua into the Promised Land, the Lord gave Joshua key instructions. "Be strong and courageous," God told him, "Do not be terrified; do not be discouraged, for the Lord your God will go with you wherever you go" (Joshua 1:9).

I believe this Scripture gives us the best definition of courage. I've seen many definitions for the word, but none better than this: one's awareness that God is with them.

Of course, none of us can be God for our spouse, so our presence won't have the effect that His does, but many good effects do come from our being there for our spouse. Courage is certainly one of them, as are security, feeling loved, feeling supported, knowing that someone cares enough to lend us their time and attention, confidence that we don't have to fight this battle alone, and knowing someone is there should we need their words or actions.

## Helping

I grew up on a tobacco farm in North Carolina. I remember more than a few times when some threat would befall other farmers in our community, things like flooding, damage from hail, or more poundage than they could harvest by season's end. In those times, my dad would have us all go over with our equipment and entire crew and work to get them out of the trouble they were in.

We would temporarily neglect our own crop to help the ones in the unusual situation, and my dad would provide the emergency service completely gratis for the friend in dire need, while still paying our crew members for their time and purchasing the necessary fuel and supplies needed to carry out the work. My dad wasn't the only farmer so generous to his fellows; the entire community operated by the motto *a friend in need is a friend indeed.*

> **Don't just have a friend, be one.**

Maybe that's what Jesus meant when He told the parable of the good Samaritan, although the prompting question was, "Who is my neighbor?" I've always taken the parable's lesson to be: *Don't just have a friend, be one.*

That's the attitude that'll work best for spousal friendship. In all the counseling Sharlene and I have done with couples having marriage trouble, the most common problem we've seen is spouses' unwillingness to focus on their own responsibility, drumming away, instead, at their spouse's. Once they turn the corner and make the change in perspective of taking responsibility, everything changes. The shift in direction and momentum at that point is undeniable. Our counseling sessions take off and become celebratory. It often isn't easy, but when it happens, we always congratulate the couple or individual for doing the difficult, critical work. They gain priceless wisdom and an invaluable skill, and we watch the couple's marriage change completely. Very satisfying and inspiring, and it's all because somebody learned to be a better spouse-friend by being a helper rather than demanding to be helped.

When God created Adam and saw that it wasn't good for him to be alone, He made a helpmate suitable for him. I like the word helpmate. The compound word makes it clear—or should—that Eve was not subordinate or inferior to Adam; *mate* implies *equal partner*.

Yet tradition has placed the wife beneath the husband. While it's true that she is called to submit to her husband, he is called to love her as Christ loved the church, giving His life for her. I dare you to love as Christ did without seriously submitting yourself. And let's not forget a primary title given to the Holy Spirit of God—the Helper. Helping is not being inferior but, I dare say, it makes one superior in the economy of God's kingdom, where the humble is exalted, the meek inherits the earth, the least is the greatest, and the last is first.

**Intercession**
Praying for someone is largely underrated and undervalued. We often say or hear things like, *When you've done everything else, pray.* We often see prayer as a last resort. There's even a football play dubbed the hail Mary. Even though I don't advocate praying to Mary, I understand that play is used as a last-ditch effort in a dire situation. That's not how prayer should be viewed by believers in Jesus.

While I recovered from a stroke a few years ago, I would often have friends tell me they were praying for me. Every time I heard those words, I felt an inexpressible gratitude in my heart.

Sharlene has read *The Power of a Praying Wife* and implemented its suggested practices, much to my benefit and appreciation to her. A significant part of my prayer life is walking trails as I talk and think with the Lord. So very often, God directs my prayers to intercede for my wife, as well as naming qualities of hers for which I'm thankful.

Nate and Haley, our son and his wife, returned from their honeymoon to learn that Haley had a brain tumor, which doctors deemed inoperable and gave a most hopeless prognosis. Our family and Haley's, along with all their friends and friends of friends, set out to both pray and enlist everyone they could to help pray for Haley to be healed. Haley's mom had been an admissions representative for a Christian college and had relationships with hundreds of churches on whom she called to solicit intercession for Haley. There were hundreds of thousands of people around the world praying that God would remove the tumor.

Nate and Haley sought out the best neuro-oncologist they could find, which was at Duke University Hospital. About six months after Haley was diagnosed, the Duke oncologist informed Haley that imaging had revealed the tumor to be gone. He had no explanation; he could now see where it had been, but it was no longer there!

God had answered the prayers of Haley, her husband, and their friends and family. Wanting to understand how God worked in situations like Haley's, I asked God, "Lord, did you heal Haley because so many people were praying for her? Is that what You require, a lot of people?"

"No," I heard the Lord say, "I like to involve as many people as possible in what I do for My children."

It may be that there's no stronger, closer, better way to be involved with our spouse than by interceding for them.

### Lifting

Good friends give each other a lift whenever and in whatever way it's needed. Jesus knew that the church needed Him to lift them into position and condition. As Ephesians 5:27 tells us, He lifted us into existence and continues by His Spirit to lift us into purity so that He may present us to Himself in eternity. God calls us friend, and Jesus is that friend that is closer than a brother. As the consummate friend-groom, Jesus gave His life to provide for us the lift we most need, to be presented as His eternal bride.

In keeping with Jesus' model, there will be sacrifice required to lift each other in various ways, but they're sacrifices we can make while we go on living with our friend-spouse. The emotional lifts into peace and joy, the lift into confidence and self-esteem, and the boost of faith usually will involve sacrifices of time, attention, thought, and words. When physical help is needed, some bodily exertion may be the requisite sacrifice.

At various times I've needed lifts in confidence that I can accomplish something, lifts in faith to remember to trust God, lifts in self-esteem to pull me out of depression, and lifts physically to tackle things I couldn't achieve by myself. All these liftings I've received from my spouse.

> It may be that there's no stronger, closer, better way to be involved with our spouse than by interceding for them.

Jesus was constantly lifting people as He healed them (lifting physically) and taught them (lifting them mentally), but the greatest lift He delivered mankind was when He forgave them. Forgiving is perhaps the most powerful example we can follow. Jesus' removing the sin burden we carried lifted us to the place of fellowship with God, making us spiritually as light as a feather, thus Jesus' claim that His burden is light. And we always have the open opportunity to lighten the burdens of both our spouse and ourself by forgiving them when our spouse needs it.

> **Forgiving is perhaps the most powerful example we can follow.**

Forgiveness coming from our best friend, our spouse, is tremendously lifting, having been relieved of the burden of guilt and impossible indebtedness. And, of course, forgiveness always carries the bonus of the forgiver being unburdened. As Corrie Ten Boon said, "To forgive is to set a prisoner free and discover the prisoner was you."

Friends forgive; best friends forgive quickly; spouses' most powerful best-friend gesture may well be forgiving. A marriage replete with forgiveness is the closest thing to a perfect marriage that there ever could be. Of all the lifting a couple can do for each other, forgiving is the most effective because it's what we need most.

**Empathy**
Empathy is when one shares in the feelings of another. Empathy is totally scriptural, stated most concisely in Romans 12:15—*Rejoice with those who rejoice; mourn with those who mourn.* In fact, the Bible calls for us to do as Jesus typically did

and go a major step beyond what was previously expected, spurring us on to share in action (rejoice and mourn) as well as feelings (happiness and sadness).

One of the marks of close friends is that they know each other so well and care for one another so deeply that they are very keen to pick up on the feelings each other is experiencing. A husband and wife can and should have this level of closeness. In married couples I've seen such a closeness that they think alike, make identical gestures, and share like thought processes. I've experienced this with my wife as well. This occurs when two people identify so profoundly with each other that their unity grows as deep as two gigantic trees with tap roots. It's as if their roots are intertwined, and they're being fed from the same stream and pool of nutrients. This may be another way of saying they're one flesh. When a married couple is truly unified sexually, emotionally, mentally, and spiritually, each is going to feel some of the things going on internally with the other.

First Corinthians 2 communicates what it's like to have the Holy Spirit dwelling within us. Paul writes that the only way one can know the thoughts of another is for person A's spirit to be in person B. That, Paul explains, is what has happened with God being person A and every believer being person B. This is how God has revealed mysteries to us in this age. It's how He conveyed His Word to writers of the New Testament, and how He helps us other believers understand Scripture and receive direction for our lives.

Spirit-filled marriage partners also have a great advantage in this way. The husband has within him the Spirit of God, as does the wife. So, they both have the same Spirit in them, which is huge, even necessary, in achieving marital unity, but it's even more than that. The couple also loves each other with such deep phileo love that it's as if their spirits (or their hearts) are intertwined. With such unity of spirit, there's a whole lot of perceiving of each other's feelings going on.

Empathy, for the married couple, is the next level compared to any other relationship. It's only in the marriage where all four loves can be present. But I'm getting ahead of myself (we'll dive deeper into this when we get to eros love). Now, let's return to phileo, the friendship love.

Paul mentions in Colossians 2 the idea of believers being knit together in love. This is what I picture when phileo-empathy is happening with a married couple. The two best friends' hearts are knit together by the love they share for each other. So, their bond makes empathy—something elusive to other less intimate relationships—happen naturally.

## Offering

I had a friend ask me for a loan recently. Since I had loaned him money before, he wanted to repeat the lending transaction process. However, I suspected that this time, since his income had really taken a hit, he'd have trouble paying back a loan while meeting his regular expenses. I realized he didn't need a loan but rather, a gift. I told him he could have the money, but he didn't need to pay me back, that it was a gift, not a loan.

This is another thing good friends do for one another—offer them what they really need. The stratospheric example is God meeting our single greatest need by offering His Son without our earning, deserving, or being required to repay His offering.

This done between spouses is essentially agape love showing up in the context of marriage interwoven with phileo love. Two factors are involved in an agape-phileo offering: it meets a real need, and no retribution is required. So, I'll-do-this-for-you-if-you-do-that-for-me doesn't qualify. Those agreements can be fine, but they aren't the same as a no-strings-attached offering from one spouse to another.

Jesus taught us that He desires for us to give to those who cannot pay us back, invite those who'll never throw a party of their own and reciprocate with an invitation to us. It's another nuance to grace that He was teaching—that we need to apply unmerited favor in any way we can think of.

The offering factor in phileo love between spouses incapsulates grace; it interweaves phileo with agape. The typical way of husband and wife should be that of perpetual non-compensated offerings to one another. What a beautiful and peaceful marriage that is!

**Intensity of Phileo Love**

A trait typical in friendship is an intensity of love for one another. The level of desire for presence, helping, lifting, empathy, and offerings by one to the other is a pretty good indication of the strength of the friendship. It's among the most vital signs for a marriage, although all four loves should have strong intensity. Spouses who aren't passionate about the six parts of P-H-I-L-E-O are unlikely to remain best friends until they become more passionate about their friend and friendship.

As kids, we practically begged our parents at times to let us be with our best friend, to have a sleepover at either their house or ours. And we were excitedly engaged in one or more of the P-H-I-L-E-O parts of friendship, although most of us probably didn't intercede for them in prayer very much, but not because our friendship lacked intensity; we just lacked the spiritual maturity as kids to be effectual in our prayer life.

If the friendship part of a marriage relationship needs improvement, lacking passion and intensity, it's best remedied by investing time, attention, and effort in doing things together.

As I've stated earlier, Sharlene and I do something special for our anniversary every year. Additionally, we go on dates once or twice a week, have most nights at home alone together, and designate one day or evening a month to taking a walk (on the beach or on nature trails) to talk about and pray for our relationship. These commitments keep our marriage strong and fend off trouble that would threaten our friendship.

# ⁓9⁓

# Storge Love in Marriage

The Lord could've brought the family about in any order He chose. But Cain and Abel came after their parents. This made marriage the priority chronologically. He didn't create in the order, Adam, Cain, Abel, and Eve, but rather, Adam, Eve, Cain, and Abel. This order speaks to the order priority He gives to family relationships. The marriage is first, then the parent-child, then the sibling relationship.

Not only is the order of creating the first family significant, but so is the manner. While the children came from both the father and mother, the wife was formed from an actual part of the husband's body. Thus, Adam's declaration, *flesh of my flesh and bone of my bone*. The children were produced, not from a part of the parents' body but from what their bodies produced. Sperm and ovaries are different from rib bone just as saliva is different from the tongue. So, the natural connection of Adam and Eve was so strong that God considered the two as one flesh.

But God didn't limit the status of oneness to the inaugural couple, for He immediately established a timeless principle for all married couples, saying that a man, therefore, would leave his parents, which Adam didn't have, and intertwine himself with his wife. I admit, the word intertwine is an *Interwoven Love* term, as opposed to the one used in Genesis, but it aptly depicts the fused, indivisible connection God desires for husband and wife. If you prefer, Scripture's word choice is "cleave," which means to attach permanently.

Let's look at the major points of the creation of Adam and Eve to better understand storge and the married couple.

First, God makes the couple in the image of the Godhead, which is Father, Son, and Holy Spirit. Jimmy Evans illustrates this very effectively by having three people join him on the stage. These three people stand closely together with arms around each other. They represent the Godhead—three in one. Then Jimmy invites a husband-wife couple up. He has the husband stand by himself, apart from his wife. Jimmy shows the audience that the one man is not in the image of the Godhead. Then he brings the husband and wife together, has them stand with arms around each other, and points out that the couple is still not in the image of the Godhead. Then he goes and stands with the married couple, he in the middle with arms around both and explains that he represents God. Thus, a married couple with God in the center of their relationship is what He had in mind when He endeavored to create mankind in His (or Their) image.

God's purpose for creating two married people, Adam and Eve, was that the wife would help the husband accomplish what neither of them could accomplish alone. The marriage is perhaps the best example of the principle of exponential power in godly partnership, which is that one can chase a thousand and two can chase ten thousand. Stated in Deuteronomy 32:30, this principle describes what two people can do together when God is with them. A married couple surrendered to God will exhibit exponential power when they work together. God certainly had this in mind in His idea of marriage.

God didn't neglect the assignment of roles when He

created marriage. From the onset, He cast the wife as helpmate and the husband as head. This arrangement is disturbing to many on the surface; but once they get beneath the surface to better understand God's meaning, it's much more palatable. The word "helpmate" is telling—a helper may seem subservient but only to a superior, not to a mate; spouses are mates, not superior-inferior. And we should remember that God calls Himself (the Holy Spirit) our Helper. Lest we see the husband's headship as supporting of male dominance, Jesus clarified that leaders in His kingdom are the ones who serve, and positions of leadership are reserved for the lowliest. Paul added that husbands are to love their wives as Christ loves the church and sacrificed His life for her.

An accurate understanding of leadership in God's economy alleviates any fear that the husband should ever assume superiority or dominance over the wife or that the wife should lie down to be walked on like a doormat. To really understand the kind of wife God admires, see Proverbs 31:10 through the end that lists traits whose common themes are initiative, entrepreneurship, independence, and industriousness. Clearly God's vision for wives includes their personal fulfillment as they lovingly serve their families and communities. His plan for husbands is that they be humble and lead in the tough things, like first-to-forgive and setting examples of self-sacrifice.

God instructs husbands to leave their parents and cleave to their wives, a requirement the wife needs to also meet. This necessitates an exclusive oneness as in no other human relationship. It's a departure from the previous storge arrangement and creation of a new one, as the couple exit one household and enter another. Life becomes different, parents are reprioritized, and new top spots are created for spouses.

The final point we must get from God's establishing of

Adam and Eve's marriage we get by inference, rather than direct example. The goal and purpose of obedient living the first couple botched miserably, just as all us married couples have at times in some way. But God's plan was that the first husband and wife would help each other walk in obedience, not sin; in freedom, not in indulgence in the forbidden; in life and blessing, not death and curse. Obviously, God's plan wasn't executed in the Garden, but with His help, we modern era married couples can walk out a different story.

The New Testament provides one exemplary couple for us to examine and imitate in some ways. There aren't many godly couples revealed in the New Testament narrative, and we have to analyze this one closely to glean a good lesson, but it's worth the effort. Aquila and Priscilla were a couple who worked closely with Paul and strengthened the disciples in the early church, including the gifted speaker, Apollos, to give him a more accurate and complete understanding of Jesus and the gospel. They took Paul on as a business partner too, with his making and selling tents to help fund his ministry. After a history of the Israelites' polygamy, male dominance, and divorce, Aquila and Priscilla provide a refreshing example of a married couple working together lovingly to achieve godly accomplishments.

Peculiar to marriage, compared to the other family relationships, is the dire need for it. There can be children without siblings and married couples without children, but God was very concerned that the man would be without a suitable partner. Yes, people often pull off single parenting very well and disunited couples innovatively figure out co-parenting and can even prove themselves amicable. But none of these are God's ideal, and I assert that His grace is what makes these less ideal situations work so well, whether those involved are aware of His grace in their situations or not.

Marriage, when done God's way, is the best arrangement for partnership. The marriage bond is so naturally strong that the state recognizes the spouse as primary decision-maker when a spouse can't make their own decisions and as first recipient of executor powers for a spouse's estate when they are deceased. The most important purpose on earth for partnership is parenting. If we think outside the box, we can understand that God could have created any system He wanted to bring forth and bring up children. He could've had the stork bring babies from a designated place on earth to people related by some way other than marriage. But He established procreation and child rearing to be accomplished through husband-wife sexual connection and partnership as parents, respectively.

Storge represents the unique love family members have for each other. A married couple form the co-leadership arrangement for a family's structure. Think of a family household as being like a non-profit corporation. Every corporation wants to be profitable, but non-profit ones don't take their profits out of the company; they keep profits within the company for continued use. A family wants to be productive, and it may and should be generous to meet needs outside the family. But the real profit a family produces—edification of one another—is obviously purposed for internal use by its members. Husband and wife are like the officers of a corporation. They work together to carry out its vision, leading the other members of the family-household in the operations of the company.

God leads each married couple in establishing their unique vision. The experience of getting God's vision as a married couple helps keep the couple unified with each other and in step with the Lord. When husband, wife, and God are on the same page, the marriage is at its best. God has plans and dreams for every couple, and He always requires the couple's unified submission to Him to fulfill His vision. Proverbs 29 tells us that a people who do not know and follow God's revealed vision will have trouble in their future. This is a rampant problem for marriages in our day. The couple that has little to no relationship with God is ignorant of His ways, so they cannot follow them. If they are aware of some of God's marriage principles but neither submit to Him nor follow Him, they are stirring themselves up in a recipe for disaster. So, this corporate leadership duo must work with their CEO to gain His vision and seek His guidance to carry it out properly.

> **With God as the CEO of the marriage, a couple has the look and function that reflects God's idea of marriage.**

With God as the CEO of the marriage, a couple has the look and function that reflects God's idea of marriage. As with the Jimmy Evans illustration, the image reflection of God by mankind is made complete in the married couple functioning as leaders of the family-household.

The CEO co-leaders' relationship in a marriage entity will also look like no other company, institution, or entity in the universe. Marriage is unique because it relates a man and woman to God in a more intimate way than any other entity can.

The flow chart of a marriage is also different from any other entity. With any company, the CEO would be alone at the top of the chart. Authority would flow from them to the leader or leaders directly under them. It would continue its flow from the leader(s) down to and through the leaders directly under them, and from there it would continue to flow all the way through the authority structure to the point of delivery of the most basic work.

The family flow chart has the CEO sharing every position in the entity with every person in the entity. However, the leaders directly under the CEO are the husband and wife, and they, along with the CEO, share a oneness that cannot be found in any other type of relationship. The co-leaders and the CEO function as one, both husband and wife in submission to the desires of the CEO.

God, in His CEO role in our marriages, is a leader like none anyone has ever seen. Micromanagement is usually perceived as a negative, but God is the exception. He micromanages with gentle, loving kindness. Micromanagement is needed in only two situations. One is when workers need close accountability because they haven't proven they can succeed without it and their work is too important to allow them to fail. The second is when workers haven't yet been sufficiently trained and micromanagement serves as their training wheels. The difference between God and human managers has to do with both love and ability. No person has the ability to help in the way that God does. He, being Spirit, can involve Himself in the most intricate details in the most intimate ways. He can speak the same wise counsel to the hearts of both husband and wife at the same time.

In 1997, when I was thirty-five years old and Sharlene and I had five of our six children, I longed desperately to leave my career track in healthcare administration and go into full-time evangelistic ministry as a preacher and musician. Sharlene was not onboard with this move, but I knew that, if I were going to do it, she had to be with me in it. One Thursday night, I went for a walk in our neighborhood. "Lord," I prayed as I walked, "I believe this move is right. But I can't do this without Sharlene's partnership. If You're leading me in this, please speak the same thing to her." I decided to say nothing else to Sharlene, to give God space to work.

The following Monday evening, four days after my prayer walk, I was standing in the kitchen after work, reading the paper. Sharlene walked in from the carport and put her bag down. She lifted her eyes to mine and simply said, "Gabe, I think you need to go into full-time ministry." Obviously, I wanted to know what changed her mind. Working for her dad at the time, Sharlene had spent some time at work looking over some historical family documents. She'd discovered that she had some very successful ancestors, a publishing tycoon, among other business people who had attained high levels of accomplishment and wealth. Yet, she'd never heard of any of them, even though they were her family. "I just thought," she said, "what is this life unless you give it away?"

Joy flooded my heart like the deluge of Noah's day. The CEO of our household had connected Sharlene's and my hearts with His to walk in His vision for us!

I've heard it said that marriage is not addition but multiplication. It stands to reason. With a God-filled power couple, accomplishment isn't made at the rate of addition but of multiplication. God said that His presence unified with His people would result in one person putting to flight a thousand enemies, and two would put ten thousand to flight. Addition would have totaled two thousand, but this economy includes a multiplier of ten, not the addition of one. This system applies to marriage, God's most foundational human relationship.

And yet, multiplication works in reverse when the reverse is more favorable, because grace is all about favor. One spouse multiplied by one spouse equals one tightly, powerfully unified couple; one times one is one. Further, one times one times one is also one. So, a spouse times a spouse times God equals an even more tightly and powerfully unified marriage partnership. This equation is immensely powerful.

Sharlene and I own a property just outside Wilmington, North Carolina, that includes our home and several other buildings on five-and-a-half acres with a pond and a lovely combination of wooded and grassy land. For all of the fifteen years we've owned it now, we've felt that God wanted us to use it to reach and disciple people for Jesus. We've launched *Marriage Club*, a small group of couples that meets monthly for fellowship dinner and discussion-based study around a marriage topic, followed by prayer for the needs of the group and marriages in our community.

We also hold retreats from time to time; we've hosted marriage retreats and leadership retreats for ministry leaders, and we plan to expand our retreat schedule. We plan to launch a discipleship ministry for boys in January of 2025 called Royal Rangers; we'll use our property for classroom training and for the outdoor living skills that Royal Rangers includes.

All these ministry efforts are part of the vision Sharlene and I believe God has called us to. He's allowed us to participate and experience satisfying success in affecting people's lives with God's love and power. What a wonderful feeling to know that, with God's help, Sharlene and I can enjoy such important accomplishments!

The common thread running through both agape and storge is love-is-not-proud. I've had the opportunity to lead several skilled nursing facilities, a. k. a. nursing homes. Having a good Director of Nursing is vital for the success of a nursing center. All of the DONS I've worked with have had varying degrees of success, their success always commensurate with the humility-honesty factor with which they worked.

I've noticed that the best corporate leaders, regardless of the type or size of the company, possess the honesty-humility combo, and those lacking either (and it may be impossible to have humility without honesty) never do well. Non-profit or for profit, large or small, faith-based or not, leaders, by my observation, will fail miserably or succeed wildly depending on the presence or absence of honesty-humility.

The husband and wife being the co-leaders of the family, honesty and humility are musts for the success of their marriage and their household. Where honesty is missing, so soon will trust be, and without trust, a marriage will stumble and fall. The success of a household can never be stronger than its marriage, the marriage being the foundation on which the household stands.

## Intensity of Storge Love

The love we have for our family members we're biologically kin to is, in my opinion, an organic love. We find ourselves naturally drawn to our blood kin because we have something very strong connecting us—genetics. Like my pastor said to me, blood is thick. Most of us have great interest in our ancestry; it tells us something about ourselves because natural family has an intense connection.

The husband-wife relationship needs the same or stronger intensity as the genetically connected family relationships. The husband and wife have the roles of leading their household, so the intensity of their connection is most important; if they falter, so does the family.

Families are usually more or less unified in proportion to the time they spend together. I saw this in my family. When my mom was alive, she was the hub that guaranteed us all getting together for birthdays, holidays, and family traditions. However, after Mom passed away, my siblings and I had to make a great effort to keep those traditional gatherings going.

The husband and wife don't have the advantage of natural

family relationship; rather, theirs is by law, by covenant, and by choice. So, husband-wife, in as much need for strength of unity as any other relationship type, must take measures to intensify their storge love.

Just as my siblings and I made extra effort to keep our family bond strong, and as families hold family reunions many generations after their patriarch and matriarch have passed away, husband and wife need to hold their own reunions.

Couples can have date nights and take trips together or whatever it takes to keep the bonds of their familial love strong. I accepted an interim healthcare administrator position four hours from home; this was my third distant interim job over a two-year period. I, being a person who craves alone time, would sometimes go days without talking to my wife. We would talk and text on an as-needed basis, and there were days when there was no issue we needed to discuss.

Sharlene, the type of person who needs more human interaction than I do, told me that, going into this third interim situation, we needed to talk every day, even if just to say hello and catch up on each other's day. That's what it took for us to keep our storge love strong, so that's what we did. It worked for us, but every couple needs to figure out for themselves how to stay united and keep their storge love's intensity level healthy and strong.

> Every couple needs to figure out for themselves how to stay united and keep their storge love's intensity level healthy and strong.

# ⤙10⤚

## Eros Love in Marriage

There's often a natural disconnect between a person's idea of God and the intense pleasure that comes with sex. Sex feels so good that there must be something wrong about it, something that wouldn't be pleasing to God. That view comes from a misunderstanding of who God is and not realizing that sex, with all its wonder, really was His idea.

A man and woman have sex. Their foreplay is so enjoyable they can scarcely believe they're experiencing it. It's everything they imagined it would be and more. They're keenly aware that sex is the most enjoyable experience available to mankind. They end up lying beside each other, reflecting on what they just experienced together; all the nerves throughout their bodies were carrying a heavier weight of pleasure than they ever thought possible. Mentally they were and still are so stimulated that they feel completely overwhelmed in the best way. Their emotions have them so overjoyed that they believe they're more privileged than anyone could have ever been.

In that moment, the last thing they want to consider is God and what He thinks of them. Pleasure to that magnitude and a holy God cannot be compatible. He's the judge of all sin; how could He not judge what they just did as taboo on some level?

What's missing is a familiarity with God. The married couple that knows God, both people having an eternal relationship with Him and a deeply personal walk with Him, interpret their sexual experience completely differently. Whereas couple A (the one unfamiliar with God) view God as distanced from and unapproving of their sex life, couple B actually includes God— as the one who created sex and presents it as a gift at each time the couple has intimate time together—in their pleasurable experience, understanding that He is indeed pleased with them as they enjoy the amazing gift He's created for them. Couple B finds themselves thinking thoughts of gratitude to God, first, for what they are enjoying, and then later, for the increased intimate pleasure-filled connection they now have as a result.

As the Greeks used the word, eros was strictly sexual love. We get the word erotic from it, and if we don't move beyond its original Greek meaning, it could include a casual hookup, an orgy, porn, or any sexual act between any two people with morality as a non-factor. That usage coming so far short of what God has in mind for marriage, there must be more to it if we're going to make use of the word and what it represents in a godly way. Its ungodly meaning is doubtless the reason it found no place in Scripture. So, I add to its original meaning the qualities needed for a husband and wife to be pleasing to God; through agape-grace intertwined with eros, they can have a sex life that's pleasing to God and edifying to their marriage.

God's invention of sex and marriage produced something pure, right, perfect, and holy. The world's mentality of leaving God out of sex perverts it. To pervert means to turn something a complete 180 degrees from God's intention for it (*per* = thorough, or all the way; *vert* = turn). The word

> God's invention of sex and marriage produced something pure, right, perfect, and holy.

79

repent means to essentially do the opposite of pervert. They both mean to turn 180 degrees, but pervert is to *turn away* from God while repent is to *turn back* to God. So, our sex life can be either perverted or bearing fruit of repentance.

At the heart of eros' meaning, there will be connection—intimate connection. The intimate connection factor is present in eros' original Greek use, yet it can include sexual sin. So, there must be more to it for the godly married couple; otherwise, the marriage bed wouldn't differ much from the bed of sexual immorality. And anyone familiar with God understands that isn't His vision for the sexual life of a married couple.

All the forms of sexual immorality share, at their core, the element of selfishness. And if it isn't mutual selfishness, it's dominance by one partner, typically the male, although the female can assume that sexually dominant, controlling role too, more often by coercion and less often by intimidation. It goes without saying that neither dominance nor mutual selfishness has place in the sex life God envisions for married couples. The intertwining of agape love with eros essentially sanctifies it. The marriage bed's quality of being undefiled necessitates for it to include agape, not merely the fact that a couple had a wedding ceremony.

These points being made, we will use a new term, holy eros. Holy eros is eros intertwined with agape, transforming human sexual love to take on God's intended beauty by intertwining it with the love He has for us.

*Holy* means *set apart*. God Himself is set apart from all others. He is unique in the best way. He is higher, wiser, more powerful, and more loving than any other. Holiness is a significant part of His character and identity. He sets us Jesus followers apart from the non-believing world. He wants us to be holy as He is holy.

My parents never used timeout as a means of correction; the belt was their only tool, unless they used a switch when we were outside. Sharlene and I did use timeout for our kids in addition to spanking. We had them sit in a certain chair in a certain corner with no talking, playing, or laughing, timeout was being separated from all things fun. Holiness isn't like timeout.

When I was playing with my friends and misbehaved, sometimes, to spare me the embarrassment of a public spanking, my mom would have me come sit with her while my friends continued to play. Sitting with my mom may be a step closer to what holiness is, because holy means being set apart with God, but holiness is still more than that.

Holiness is being in fellowship with God, having His counsel for decision-making, His encouragement for accomplishment, and His comfort in pain. Holy eros is sex and romance set apart with God, with God's counsel, vision, and guidance. He designed holy eros and wants to help us take full advantage of its purpose and benefits.

If we read ancient Greek writings including the word eros, it would not mean holy eros, since eros love isn't holy until it is adjusted and aligned with God's plan for sex. But it's important for us that everything that happens in the bed and the process leading into the bed meets the description of 1 Corinthians 13.

I also include in holy eros, not just the intimate physical connection, but the intimate connections in an emotional sense, as well as a spiritual

**It's important for us that everything that happens in the bed and the process leading into the bed meets the description of 1 Corinthians 13.**

81

sense. To ignore the emotional in favor only of the physical sacrifices a huge part of what holy eros should be for a couple. Indeed, intense fulfillment takes place on an emotional level for the couple taking a healthy holy eros approach to their life of sex and romance.

To use the phrase sex and romance, which I prefer, draws into the picture everything that has to do with the before, during, and after the intimate time together in bed. The romance part is de-sanctified (or perverted) by the world as much as the sex part is. The songs, movies, novels, and TV series put out by the world of pop culture presents a very different picture of romance than what God desires for it, the biggest difference being the absence of agape love and a commitment to God.

By spiritual intimacy in sex and romance, I'm referring to the most inner part of a person, who they really are, the part that is eternal; some may call it the soul or heart connection. I'm using the word "spiritual."

There is something deeply spiritual that happens between two people when they have sex, no matter the type of relationship, or lack thereof, the two people have. Paul wrote that even a prostitute becomes one flesh with her customer through sex (1 Corinthians 6:16). But the spiritual connection sex makes for spouses surrendered to God and each other ties them together as husband-wife and as brother-sister-friends in Christ in a most special and godly way.

What happens in the physical is symbolic of what's happening in the spiritual, similar to water baptism being symbolic of the spiritual cleansing God does when He baptizes us by His Spirit into His new life, kingdom, and family. As the couple having sex has made their bodies bare for each other, they have also made bare their souls, presenting themselves as vulnerably exposed in the most personal and intimate way.

Further vulnerability is offered when the man enters the woman physically. They are both holding nothing back physically but exposing every part of their bodies to each other, making their bodies' greatest fragility precariously exposed. Similarly, the couple being the closest physically to each other that they could possibly be—the man inside the woman and the woman receiving into herself the man—their bodies are an outward symbol of the connection they're making spiritually, each allowing the other into their very most private spiritual space. They look into each other's eyes during their sexual connection and, the eye being the window to the soul, they connect with a depth that cannot happen any other way.

Genesis 6 describes a time very different from ours. There were "sons of God" on the earth in that era; the Hebrew word is Nephilim which some, including myself, understand as referring to fallen angels. These beings were rebels against God, so God certainly didn't intend for them to marry human women. They did just that, however, and the offspring they produced were the giants of Scripture and likely the basis for the mythological heroes like Odysseus and Hercules. Some believe that Goliath and other giants of his era were a remnant of the Nephilim seed.

The sexual connection the Nephilim had with their human wives produced such evil, along with mankind's general rebellion against God, that God decided to judge the whole world and restart humanity through Noah's three sons and his sons' wives. This Genesis 6 account is so strange to us modern readers that most of us understand little of it. One of the most obvious takeaways is that God cares greatly about earthly sexuality.

In the chapter *Love's Fabric in the*

**God cares greatly about earthly sexuality.**

*Life of Jesus,* I likened the eros love a man and woman have to God giving His Spirit to us believers. By His giving us His Spirit to dwell in the most inner part of us, He's making the most intimate connection possible. For the married couple, sex is the most intimate connection possible in physical, spiritual, and emotional senses. Just as we miss out on opportunities for intimacy with God when we quench the Spirit (the biggest consequence of sin for believers), the married couple misses out on intimate connection opportunities (the greatest benefit of sex, along with producing offspring) with each other by neglecting their sex and romance life.

The benefits of a healthy, active holy eros life for the married couple are an intimate connection, a most pleasurable mutual experience, and protection from sexual immorality.

We all have fond memories of good times with the people in our lives. My siblings and I swam together in the river on hot summer days as a break from our farm work. We still talk about those times we spent as teenagers and preteens now in our fifties and sixties. Those fun and pleasurable times helped form a bond among us that cannot be broken. Swinging out onto the river waters on a rope hanging from a tree, playing keep away in the water, and our mom reminding us to take a bar of soap so we could make our daily bath part of the swimming ritual that brought us closer together.

Sex and romance are, for a husband and wife, just such a bonding part of marriage, depositing into their intimacy bank memories of pleasurable times together that will never be erased. My siblings and I share other past experiences we discuss only within our sibling circle. A husband and wife also hold an exclusive history of experiences they keep between themselves; they're too personal to share with others. A strong bond is formed by experiences shared only between husband

and wife. Sex and romance provide this great benefit for the married couple.

Unlike phileo and storge, eros has its own set of actions; it's more than just a scope through which to apply agape. Yet, none of its attitudes or actions must conflict with agape; the two loves can fit together like hand and glove.

The actions of eros are those of physical-sexual affection. Intertwined with agape, they are always performed in kindness toward the other spouse, with patience for them, willing to wait on them and not give up on them when they aren't satisfying in a physical-sexual way. There is no domineering, neither is there any seeing themselves as loftier in some way than the other. Spouses in agape-eros love actions always protect each other, placing their spouse's safety, comfort, and pleasure on par with their own. They apply the Golden Rule (do for others as you want done for you). Agape-eros will be very different from the eros anyone has known without the agape qualities, yet is another wonderful reason for placing God in the center of our marriage relationships.

Vital to a vibrant and satisfying life of agape-eros is investment. One investment vehicle is attraction. Regardless of the scenario, there are four practices spouses can include in their lifestyle to keep the attraction factor healthy.

1. Invest in being attractive as a consistent piece of your lifestyle, spreading your investment to all parts of yourself, like physical, mental, social, professional, character, spiritual, etc., remembering that attraction involves the whole of a person, not just one part, like the physical.

2. Invest in being attracted to your spouse by regularly meditating on their qualities, choosing an admirable physical quality and character quality as focuses for meditating.

3. Invest in the relationship itself and the connection you have, remembering that the ultimate purpose of attraction is to support the connection you desire as a married couple. This means studying your spouse to know specific ways to connect with them, specifically, so that you can invest effectively rather than miss the mark by not understanding the ways your particular spouse connects.

4. Answer honestly and regularly this question: is it my spouse whose attraction I'm pursuing or possibly others? The attention of people other than your spouse can distract and derail your attraction building strategy, and it can happen with such subtlety that your heart can become unfaithful before you realize it.

I counseled a couple in their fifties who struggled in the sex and romance part of their marriage. The husband was frustrated because the wife had little interest in sex. The wife said she was attracted to her husband but didn't feel good about her own body, and that shut the door on her interest in sex. Even though the wife was dissatisfied with her body, the husband wasn't and was still sexually attracted to her. Wanting to help in some way, the husband asked what he could do to help open his wife's mind to the idea of having sex again. The wife told him there was nothing he could do, that it was her issue and only she could correct it. They discussed the possibility of never having sex again, but the wife insisted that would be unfair to the husband since his desire for sex was still nearly as strong as it had been in previous decades.

The wife committed to resolve her issue by changing her lifestyle, developing a better self-image, and regaining her interest in sex. The husband committed to be patient while the wife went through the process of making the change. They also agreed to, in the interim, invest in their sex and romance life by spending time together, going on dates, and working on the non-sexual part of their romantic life, like kissing, hugging, and intimate conversation while going for walks on the beach.

This was a case of the wife showing kindness and choosing to seek her husband's satisfaction over her own. The husband exercised patience and kindness by deferring to the wife's time-table over his own.

It's an example of agape love in both spouses and their attempt to interweave agape and eros for a more complete marriage. They also invested more deeply in the phileo—friendship—part of their marriage by intentionally spending more time together, which helped fill the void until they could resume their life of sexual intimacy. As a result they saw their friendship grow stronger in the process. So, this couple tightened the weaves of agape-eros and agape-phileo, strengthening their marriage in three of the four loves—agape, phileo and eros. Their storge bond was already strong; eventually, they were strong in all four loves and thereafter enjoyed a wonderful marriage. It's been a joy to witness this couple strengthen their marriage in these ways.

Two other factors that set eros apart from the other three loves are longevity and perseverance. Perseverance has to do with its ability to exist in various circumstances, and longevity pertains to its lifespan. Agape, storge, and phileo loves can and should always be active, with no reason for taking breaks, as long as a married couple are alive. Do not be weary of doing good, Paul challenged the church, and there is no good excuse for withdrawing agape love in either the family or friend relationship. Agape love always perseveres; eros does not.

From a perseverance standpoint,

**Agape love always perseveres; eros does not.**

there are times, wrote Paul, when a married couple should abstain from sex in deference to their "prayer and fasting" life. Then they should come back together in sexual intimacy, he continues; otherwise, their abstinence from one another may give way to immorality on the part of one or the other. So, Paul establishes not only that the marriage's sex life is a lower priority than its prayer life, but also the importance of being sexually active together in keeping their sex lives moral and not falling into adulterous error.

Of course, a time of prayer and fasting isn't the only reason for being sexually inactive. Just as the Bible doesn't address specifically the details of many other subjects, there are some common sense factors in holding off on sex that no biblical writer ever addressed. Obviously, if one spouse doesn't feel well, is exhausted, or is going through something emotionally challenging, only a despicable spouse would insist on having their way, expecting their struggling spouse to fall in line with their inconsiderate demands. And if one spouse is physically unable to perform sexually, their spouse needs to tap into the *love is patient* quality of agape love. On the other hand, couples who so desire can get creative and find ways to have sex in some way despite the limitations they face.

Longevity, in regard to eros, has to do with how long the couple will have a sex life, or at what point the sex life will end for the couple. It has to end at some point before they pass away, depending on their longevity of life, sexual health, and possibly other factors. But it's wise for us all to prepare ourselves for the phase in life and marriage when sex won't be an option. Notice that as I'm referring to perseverance and longevity, my focus is on sex, specifically, not the non-sexual romance part of sex and romance. I don't know of a reason a couple can't always be romantic. Also, a couple can be physically romantic with activity other than the part they cannot perform; for example, a couple can kiss and hug and do heavy petting, even if they can't "go all the way."

Much of eros is kept appropriate—made holy—by the intertwining of agape with it. It's impossible to address every single possible scenario in detail, but agape provides the structure through which we can approach all of life in the right way. As Peter wrote (1 Peter 4:8), agape love covers a multitude of sin. Coupling agape with eros is another way love covers sin; in this case, cover means prevents or precludes sexual mistreatment, including being inconsiderate of one another.

The common thread I see running through both agape and eros is twofold. First is the love-is-not-self-seeking and does-not-delight-in-evil-but-rejoices-in-the-truth qualities. The sex life is productive for the marriage only when spouses put each other before themselves.

The second fold of the common agape-eros thread is does-not-delight-in-evil-but-rejoices-in-the-truth. Truth being *the way it really is* (my definition), essentially living in reality as opposed to fantasy or denial, the agape-eros life doesn't allow romantic-sexual attention to be directed outside the marriage. The truth is that the spouses are each other's reality, and to direct attention outside the marriage is not only contrary to the truth but is evil.

A core and vital principle for Christians is that we are not conformed to this world, whose practice is to leave God out, but that we, rather, allow God to transform us by renewing our minds. Our life of love in marriage needs this principle as much as any other application in our life does. If we imitate the world's use of eros, conforming to its image in this area of our lives, it'll look starkly different from the way God intends its application by a godly married couple who intertwines it with agape. Remember that agape formed its definition by the way Jesus and the early church used it; the Greeks had no such concept without Jesus Christ giving it meaning. And eros' use by both first century Greeks and the modern Christ-rejecting world, means little more than animal-like sex.

## We must think very differently from the world around us.

Our sex and romance life is among the most critical, and perhaps difficult parts of life to which the Romans12:2 principle should apply. So, we must think very differently from the world around us. Studying, meditating on, and applying the principles of Scripture are how our minds will be renewed. Hopefully, reading and rereading *Interwoven Love* will aid in the attempt to renew our minds in this way, as well.

**Intensity of Holy Eros**
Much of this chapter has been given to keeping eros-love holy and intense. Now, as we make intensity a focus, let's remind ourselves of Jesus' ministry and connect some dots by answering some rhetorical questions.

1. Jesus died and returned to the Father so the Holy Spirit could be sent to us. What in us needs to die so that the intimate connection between us and our spouse can live stronger?
2. God gives us believers His Spirit so we can have overflowing joy. What can we give or do for our spouse in the area of sex and romance to bring them greater joy?
3. God never uses the promise of His Spirit to coerce a certain response from us. Can we commit that our spouse will be free

from any coercion or leveraging of anything we could use to selfishly bring about a response from our spouse in our sex and romance life?

Using these questions appropriately (as they are taken from God's example for us) can help keep our sex and romance life holy and intense.

**Using these questions appropriately (as they are taken from God's example for us) can help keep our sex and romance life holy and intense.**

# ~11~

## Scope and Priority

Scope and priority are two important factors to consider in the four types of love in marriage. Both are explained in this chapter. A chart for each is also included to enhance understanding.

| Scope | | |
|---|---|---|
| LOVE | SCOPE | OBJECTS |
| Agape | All | Mankind |
| Phileo | Many | Friends |
| Storge | Few | Family |
| Eros | One | Spouse |

The scope refers to the appropriate recipients of each respective type of love. Scope is key in defining the loves. In fact, phileo and storge are defined almost solely by their scope, since their love types are mostly agape being expressed to those in their scopes, the objects of their love. So, with some nuance within each type, phileo is agape expressed to friends and storge is agape being expressed to family. Eros is different; it's agape expressed to the spouse but adds to a greater extent its own specific sex and romance expressions to agape.

The scope for agape includes every person who is a part of

our lives in any way. But if we face the choice in favoring one over another in some way, the spouse is always the more favored one. For example, if we are at a gathering, it's our spouse to whom we focus our attention and favor; we agape-love all at the gathering, but our spouse is the priority object (recipient). That having to do more with priority, we'll focus on that aspect in a few paragraphs.

Phileo's scope includes all the friends we have in the world. We wouldn't consider every single human our friend; some might be acquaintances, some we don't know, and some even enemies. In terms of priority, we consider some closer friends than others, some more "dear" than others. "Best" friend is a common designation we reserve for our top priority group of friends, sometimes singling out one as our best or very best friend. If we're married, no other person should take priority status above our spouse. We may have a special bond with some friends other than our spouse; we share some unique connections with different friends because each friendship has its own history and its members have their special common interests, but when it comes to that most special place in our heart, that place is reserved for our spouse.

Storge includes in its scope all family members. Spouses are often faced with the choice of which family members they'll favor in certain situations. In fact, the love spouses have for family members other than their spouse, along with those family members' efforts to draw one away from their spouse and closer to themselves, can cloud minds for right decision-making in prioritizing.

Now let us delve into priority.

| Priority | | |
|---|---|---|
| LOVE | LOVE PRIORITY | OBJECT PRIORITY |
| Agape | 1 | Spouse |
| Phileo | 2 | Spouse |
| Storge | 3 | Spouse |
| Eros | 4 | Spouse |

Priority is ordering the loves in two different senses, each love-type compared to the others, and the objects compared within each love-type. Agape is most important because it's God's way of loving us and it's the love He's called us to have for others, especially our spouse. Agape is also what makes the other loves work effectively.

In the sense of object priority, the spouse will always take top priority in receiving our love. That's a no-brainer in theory, but theory often omits factors present in the practical; in practicing marital love, other relationships can threaten a marriage.

Perhaps the two most common threats to spouses' prioritizing appropriately come through parents and children. Siblings and friends are other common relationships through which division can threaten a marriage.

I once performed a wedding ceremony for a couple and included vows recited by the parents of the bride and the groom. I did so because I knew the bride and her parents had a relationship that could potentially be unhealthy for the marriage. Both sets of parents repeated the vows, but the bride's parents didn't keep their commitment, nor did the bride. As the couple journeyed through their marriage, the wife and her parents maintained a higher priority relationship than the wife did with her husband, the wife never having re-prioritized her parents.

After eight years of marriage, the wife chose to leave the man in favor of being closer, both emotionally and geographically, to her parents. Indeed, the parents advocated their daughter's decision after they had unintentionally sown eight years of seeds of division in their daughter's marriage. Today that couple is connected only by their co-parenting relationship; they have a son the father is trying to bring up to become an independent adult, a vision the mother seems unable to share.

Children, it seems, have a natural expertise in dividing their parents. To gain parental advocacy for their own interests, kids are gifted at finding any possible opportunity to get one parent in their corner. A parent can find themselves surprisingly in the corner of the child, looking across the ring to see their spouse in the opposite corner. When the bell rings, it's the parents who come out swinging, while the child sits pulling for the parent they've won to their cause.

It seems impossible that someone—especially a child—could achieve such an ingenious accomplishment by accident, but the child is unknowingly demonstrating the power of selfishness. It's even strong enough to deeply damage a marriage, just by finding the armor's chink that will hurt a parent and make them believe their spouse was the enemy.

Things are even more complicated and difficult with marriages of blended families, the children having unique and longer history with their original parent than with their newly acquired one.

I've also seen spouses who refused to re-prioritize their siblings after their wedding, allowing the sibling to share time and energy that rightfully belonged to their spouse.

When I was engaged to be married, a married friend emphatically made the comment, as if warning me, 'Blood is thick!' I later learned that friend and his wife were in conflict because his wife's sister was overly involved with his wife, to the point of intruding on their husband-wife time. Fortunately, I didn't need that warning, since my wife and I both went into our marriage with a good sense of family relationship priorities.

Agape has to be number one among the love types. It's the way God loves us, the way He calls us to love others and is the single most important thread in the fabric of marriage. The other loves work well only when intertwined with agape. So, as priority among the love types goes, agape is inarguably the top one. Yet the others are each uniquely vital.

The problem with prioritizing is that it's comparative. It can be that number two on the priority list is also very, very important, just not as important as number one. That's the case with phileo. Agape is always going to be top priority. Paul even wrote that it, when grouped with faith and hope—the trifecta group whose members alone will remain through the age—is the greatest; the greatest of these is agape love.

Yes, agape love is the greatest and must always be interwoven with each of the three other types of love. But phileo, the friendship of spouses, is also not expendable, nor can the marriage be strong if phileo is weak. As with agape—and all the loves—one is to choose their spouse every time as the priority recipient for phileo. Many people (all of our friends) have a place in the scope of our phileo, but we have a special category we call best friends, and then there's that one very best friend, the most special—that's the spouse. Some marriage experts ask the question, "Whom do you call first to discuss big issues, or with big news, good or bad? It should," they say, "be your spouse." I concur completely and advise couples to make their spouse the priority recipient of that call. It's a good barometer of priority within phileo. So, the second love type, phileo, must, like agape, reserve the top spot for the spouse.

Storge should take priority over eros chronologically; in other words, sex is purposed by God, its creator, for marriage, so, ideally, sex shouldn't be happening before the wedding when the couple has become officially family. In a post-Christian culture that generally leaves God out of its values and priorities, we're tasked with swimming against the tide if we're committed to a biblical Christian lifestyle. And the order of sex and marriage may prove the most contrasting of all the parts of the culture's lifestyle. More and more, couples are embracing sex before marriage, including unmarried cohabitation; even many Christian couples are electing to swim with the culture's current on this issue.

I've listed eros fourth (last) in the order of my writing about the love types, and I would judge it the lowest priority because there are some married couples who, by necessity, have little to no sex life, and their marriage can still be healthy. Yet, the couples who are able to have a vibrant life of holy eros should; if you can have it but don't, it can be detrimental to the marriage. That's how important it is, even though it's the lowest priority among the types. So, even the love type with the least priority weight, eros, can tip the marriage scales, making a marriage anything from wonderful to miserable.

In summary, the love types' priority order is: agape, phileo, storge, eros. And the spouse is top priority among all recipients of all the people in the world for every love type.

# ✕12✕

## The Fringes

At the ends of a blanket, we see fringe. The fringe is where we are now with this beautiful marriage fabric. To complete *Interwoven Love*, it seems, some help in personal application would be fitting (pardon the pun). So, please work through the following that will sew (sorry, another pun) *Interwoven Love* principles into your marriage. Each spouse, please answer for yourself, not your spouse, then let your spouse review your answers, and you can decide about your final answers after getting their input. (You may copy these charts to facilitate this exercise.)

Return to your answers after three months, see how well you followed through on your plans for improvements, and answer again all the questions to see if you've made improvements.

Finally, thank you for reading *Interwoven Love!* Godspeed as you apply its lessons in your marriage!

## Agape Love

Please fill in the open cells on the next page with your answers about your love for your spouse. Rate 1 to 5 (1=never); 5=always). Plan for improvement (if 3 or lower).

| Agape Trait | Rating | Plan for Improvement |
|---|---|---|
| I am patient. | | |
| I am kind. | | |
| I do not envy. | | |
| I do not boast. | | |
| I am not proud. | | |
| I am not rude. | | |
| I am not self-seeking. | | |
| I am not easily angered. | | |
| I keep no record of wrongs. | | |
| I always protect. | | |
| I always trust. | | |
| I always hope. | | |
| I always persevere. | | |
| I never fail to love. | | |

# Phileo Love

Please fill in the open cells with your answers about your love for your spouse. Rate 1 to 5 (1=never); 5=always). Plan for improvement (if 3 or lower).

| Phileo Trait | Rating | Plan for Improvement |
|---|---|---|
| I am good at being present for my spouse. | | |
| I'm good at helping my spouse. | | |
| I intercede for my spouse daily. | | |
| I'm good at lifting up my spouse. | | |
| I empathize deeply with my spouse consistently. | | |
| I'm generous in giving my time & resources to my spouse. | | |

# Storge Love

Please fill in the open cells with your answers about your love for your spouse. Rate 1 to 5 (1=never); 5=always). Plan for improvement (if 3 or lower).

| Storge Trait | Rating | Plan for Improvement |
|---|---|---|
| I keep God in the center of my marriage. | | |
| I work in tandem with my spouse to achieve our purpose and goals. | | |
| I fill my role as a spouse. | | |
| I live with my parents and friends in the correct priority. | | |
| I help my spouse walk in obedience to God by example & encouragement. | | |

# Eros Love

Please fill in the open cells with your answers about your love for your spouse. Rate 1 to 5 (1=never); 5=always). Plan for improvement (if 3 or lower).

| Eros Trait | Rating | Plan for Improvement |
|---|---|---|
| I keep agape intertwined with eros for my spouse. | | |
| I invest in being attractive for my spouse. | | |
| I invest in being attracted to my spouse. | | |
| I invest in the connection with my spouse (study them & focus time on them accordingly. | | |

# About the Author

Gabriel and his wife, Sharlene, will celebrate thirty-eight years of marriage in 2025. They have six children (all grown) and eight grandchildren to whom they are known as G-Pop and Lolli. Gabriel and Sharlene live in Wilmington, North Carolina, where they host Marriage Club (a small group for married and pre-married couples), marriage retreats, leadership retreats, a Royal Rangers outpost, and other ministry events on their property just outside Wilmington. They also serve as marriage counselors.

Gabriel has experience as a pastor, a healthcare administrator and a leader of missions, and is involved with local church and addiction recovery ministries. He is the author of *Brilliant Faith: Why It's Smart to Believe in Jesus* published in 2022 by River Birch Press, and his weekly blog can be found at gabrieltew.com.

The desire of Gabriel's heart is to produce resources to edify the Body of Christ and to help all his family and friends have a vibrant walk with God.